Spanish Games pack

CONTENTS
Buena Idea
Lotto en Español
Juguemos Todos Juntos

We hope you and your pupils enjoy using this compendium of 3 books. Brilliant Publications publishes many other books for teaching modern foreign languages. To find out more details on any of the titles listed below, please go to our website: www.brilliantpublications.co.uk.

100+ Fun Ideas for Practising Modern Foreign Languages in the Primary Classroom	978-1-903853-98-6
More Fun Ideas for Advancing Modern Foreign Languages in the Primary Classroom	978-1-905780-72-3
¡Es Español!	978-1-903853-64-1
Juguemos Todos Juntos	978-1-903853-95-5
¡Vamos a Cantar!	978-1-905780-13-6
Spanish Pen Pals Made Easy	978-1-905780-42-6
Lotto en Español	978-1-905780-47-1
Spanish Festivals and Traditions	978-1-905780-53-2
Buena Idea	978-1-905780-63-1
Chantez Plus Fort!	978-1-903853-37-5
Hexagonie Part 1	978-1-905780-59-4
Hexagonie Part 2	978-1-905780-18-1
C'est Français!	978-1-903853-02-3
J'aime Chanter!	978-1-905780-11-2
J'aime Parler!	978-1-905780-12-9
French Pen Pals Made Easy	978-1-905780-10-5
French Festivals and Traditions	978-1-905780-44-0
Loto Français	978-1-905780-45-7
Unforgettable French (2nd edition)	978-1-78317-093-7
Das ist Deutsch	978-1-905780-15-0
Wir Spielen Zusammen	978-1-903853-97-9
German Pen Pals Made Easy	978-1-905780-43-3
Deutsch-Lotto	978-1-905780-46-4
German Festivals and Traditions	978-1-905780-52-5
Gute Idee	978-1-905780-65-5
Giochiamo Tutti Insieme	978-1-903853-96-2
Lotto in Italiano	978-1-905780-48-8
Buon'Idea (2nd edition)	978-0-85747-696-8

Published by Brilliant Publications Limited
Unit 10
Sparrow Hall Farm
Edlesborough
Dunstable
Bedfordshire
LU6 2ES, UK

Website: www.brilliantpublications.co.uk

General information enquiries:
Tel: 01525 222292

The name Brilliant Publications and the logo are registered trademarks.

Front cover designed by Brilliant Publications Limited

Printed book ISBN: 978-0-85747-948-8
E-book ISBN: 978-0-85747-949-5

First printed and published in the UK in 2021

See the copyright pages of each individual book for the rights of the authors.

See the copyright pages of each individual book to ascertain the restrictions on reproducing pages.

Ages: 5–11yrs

Buena Idea

Time-saving Resources and Ideas for Busy Spanish Teachers

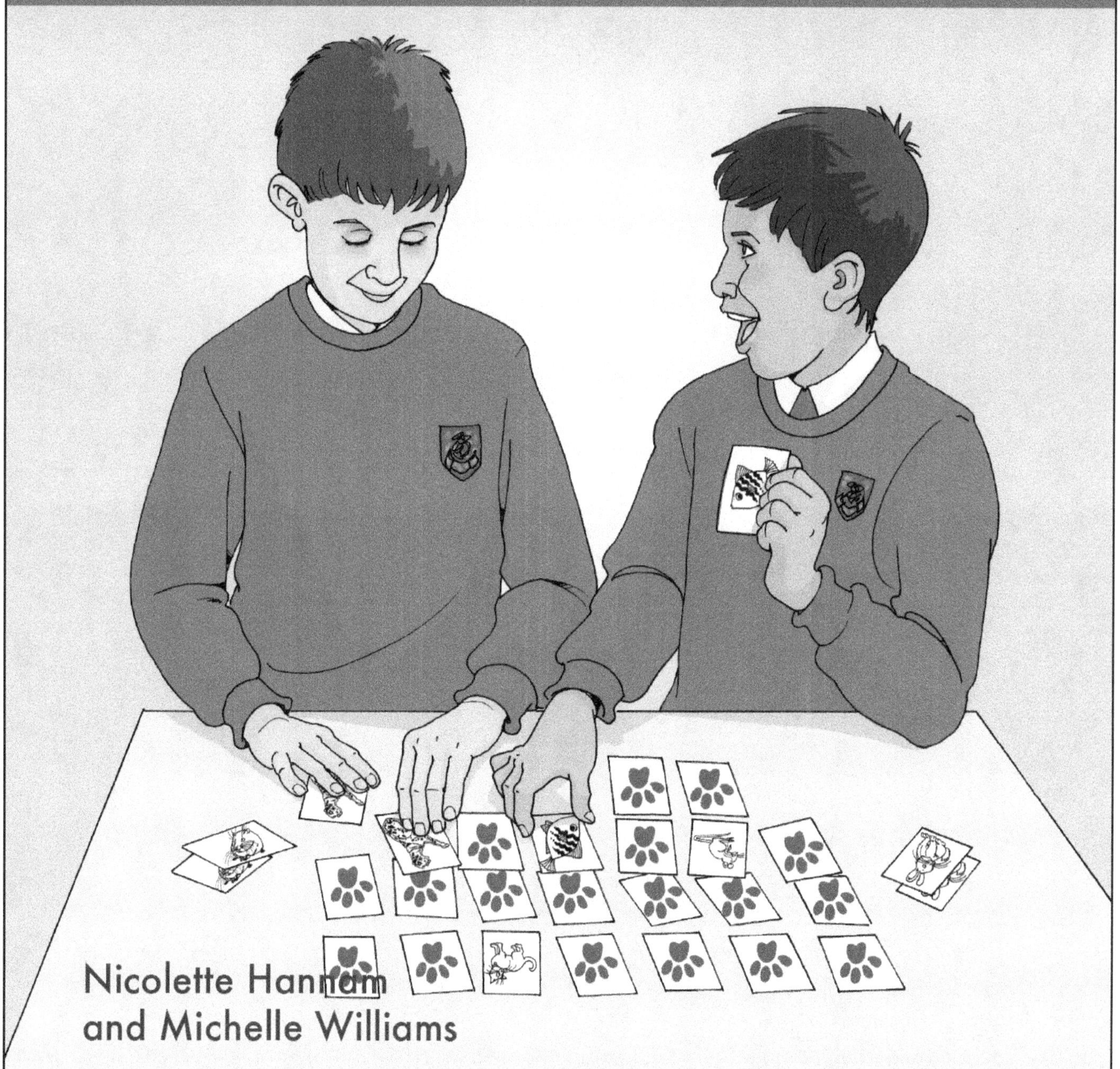

Nicolette Hannam
and Michelle Williams

Buena Idea

Time saving resources and ideas for busy Spanish teachers

Nicolette Hannam and Michelle Williams

We hope you and your pupils enjoy using this book. Brilliant Publications publishes many other books for teaching modern foreign languages. To find out more details on any of the titles listed below, please go to our website: www.brilliantpublications.co.uk.

100+ Fun Ideas for Practising Modern Foreign Languages in the Primary Classroom	978-1-903853-98-6
¡Es Español!	978-1-903853-64-1
Juguemos Todos Juntos	978-1-903853-95-5
¡Vamos a Cantar!	978-1-905780-13-6
Spanish Pen Pals Made Easy	978-1-905780-42-6
Lotto en Español	978-1-905780-47-1
Spanish Festivals and Traditions	978-1-905780-53-2
Chantez Plus Fort!	978-1-903853-37-5
Hexagonie Part 1	978-1-905780-59-4
Hexagonie Part 2	978-1-905780-18-1
Jouons Tous Ensemble	978-1-903853-81-8
C'est Français!	978-1-903853-02-3
J'aime Chanter!	978-1-905780-11-2
J'aime Parler!	978-1-905780-12-9
French Pen Pals Made Easy	978-1-905780-10-5
Loto Français	978-1-905780-45-7
French Festivals and Traditions	978-1-905780-44-0
Bonne Idée	978-1-905780-62-4
Unforgettable French	978-1-78317-093-7
Das ist Deutsch	978-1-905780-15-0
Wir Spielen Zusammen	978-1-903853-97-9
German Pen Pals Made Easy	978-1-905780-43-3
Deutsch-Lotto	978-1-905780-46-4
German Festivals and Traditions	978-1-905780-52-5
Gute Idee	978-1-905780-65-5
Giochiamo Tutti Insieme	978-1-903853-96-2
Lotto in Italiano	978-1-905780-48-8
Buon'Idea	978-0-85747-696-8

Published by Brilliant Publications Limited
Unit 10
Sparrow Hall Farm
Edlesborough
Dunstable
Bedfordshire
LU6 2ES, UK

General information enquiries:
Tel: 01525 222292
E-mail: info@brilliantpublications.co.uk
Website: www.brilliantpublications.co.uk

The name Brilliant Publications and the logo are registered trademarks.

Written by Nicolette Hannam and Michelle Williams
Illustrated by Catherine Ward
Designed by Bookcraft Ltd
Front cover designed by Brilliant Publications Limited

© Text Nicolette Hannam and Michelle Williams 2009
© Design Brilliant Publications Limited 2009

Printed ISBN 978-1-905780-63-1
ebook ISBN   978-1-905780-87-7

First printed and published in the UK in 2009

The right of Nicolette Hannam and Michelle Williams to be identified as the authors of this work has been asserted by themselves in accordance with the Copyright, Designs and Patents Act 1988.

Pages 5–148 may be photocopied by individual teachers acting on behalf of the purchasing institution for classroom use only, without permission from the publisher and without declaration to the Copyright Licensing Agency or Publishers' Licensing Services. The materials may not be reproduced in any other form or for any other purpose without the prior permission of the publisher.

Contents

Los números	The numbers	5
Los días	The days of the week	11
Los meses	The months	16
Mi familia	My family	22
Los colores	The colours	28
Los animales	Pets	36
En el aula	In the classroom	42
Las asignaturas	School subjects	50
La comida	Food	56
¿Qué tiempo hace?	The weather	64
El cuerpo	The body	70
Mis pasatiempos	My hobbies	78
La ropa	Clothes	86
En la ciudad	In the town	94
Mi casa	My house	102
Feliz Navidad	Happy Christmas	110
San Valentín	St Valentine's Day	118
Carnavales	Shrove Tuesday	125
Feliz Pascua	Happy Easter	133
La víspera de Todos los Santos	Halloween	141

Introduction

This book was written by a secondary and a primary school teacher to provide key vocabulary for twenty topics, and to give teachers ideas for introducing, teaching, reinforcing and extending new vocabulary. Each topic has key vocabulary, word matching cards, an activity sheet, a puzzle page, and ideas for extending learning through sentence building. Many topics also have picture cards. Using the book can support the teacher in covering many of the objectives in the **Framework for Modern Foreign Languages** using a choice of fun and lively activities.

The key vocabulary pages can be enlarged to A3 for classroom display, or photocopied and laminated as reference cards. The word and picture matching cards can be used in many ways. Lessons should begin with work on the Oracy Objectives in the **Framework** by repeating the new words after the teacher and playing some flashcard games. The children can then work in mixed ability pairs, using the photocopiable sheets from the book. They can match the words face up, then progress to matching them face down in a 'pairs' game. They could also play snap. They could glue the English words on an A3 sheet and carefully write the Spanish words next to them, or glue on the Spanish words, and draw pictures to match each word, and progress to writing the new words from memory.

The sentence building sheets can further develop the children's language skills, reinforcing vocabulary by using it in simple sentences. The suggestions work towards the Literacy Objectives in the **Framework** and will further develop children's reading and writing skills. The puzzle pages reinforce the language further in a fun way, and could also be used for homework.

Children should be encouraged to think about how they learn new vocabulary, a skill the Language Learning Strategies section of the **Framework** encourages. **Visual learners** will benefit from the matching sheets, and from drawing pictures to match. **Auditory learners** will benefit from repeating after the teacher and hearing their partner say the new words, perhaps during a game of snap. **Kinaesthetic learners** will enjoy cutting the words up and matching them. Using a variety of methods will cater for the many different learning styles in a class and ensure that confidence and ability grow alongside each other.

The Knowledge about Language section of the **Framework** encourages children to focus on their pronunciation and intonation. It is crucial that the language on the sheets is modelled by the teacher, or using a CD or Internet resource, and followed up with songs and rhymes.

We use all of the resources in this book ourselves with much success. Our pupils enjoy the challenge of learning new vocabulary and complete the guided sheets with pride and confidence. We sincerely hope that you and your pupils enjoy learning and using their new vocabulary.

Los números

Key vocabulary

0	**cero**
1	**uno**
2	**dos**
3	**tres**
4	**cuatro**
5	**cinco**
6	**seis**
7	**siete**
8	**ocho**
9	**nueve**
10	**diez**
11	**once**
12	**doce**

Vamos a contar.

We are going to count.

Los números ✂ Matching cards

1	2	3
4	5	6
uno	dos	tres
cuatro	cinco	seis

Los números ✂ Matching cards

7	8	9
10	11	12
siete	ocho	nueve
diez	once	doce

Los números

Activity sheet

Nombre: .... Fecha: ....

I can name and recognize numbers to 12 in Spanish.
Write the word for each number carefully and neatly in the grid below. Then draw the correct number of items to match. For example, write *uno* and draw one object. It can be anything you like, maybe a smiley face.

uno	seis	ocho	tres	doce	siete
....	....	....	....	....	....
dos	cuatro	nueve	cinco	once	diez
....	....	....	....	....	....

Adicional

What is the highest number that you know in Spanish? Can you write it in words?

Los números — Puzzle page

Busca las palabras en la sopa de letras.
Search for the words in the grid.

cero	d	w	o	c	h	o	x	k	u	k
uno	o	x	n	u	k	w	q	p	n	x
dos	c	w	c	c	u	a	t	r	o	l
tres	e	i	e	i	p	r	r	l	p	d
cuatro	k	d	w	n	x	k	e	q	s	o
cinco
seis	u	i	p	c	k	i	s	e	i	s
siete	c	e	r	o	u	x	w	r	e	w
ocho	i	z	k	p	h	r	p	h	t	l
nueve	u	l	x	k	n	u	e	v	e	q
diez	x	r	i	q	u	q	w	p	r	x
once
doce

Descifra los anagramas.
Put the letters in order.

nuo	uno
eteis	....
trcoua	....
ster	....
hooc	....
ocinc	....
ods	....
veeun	....
ssei	....
ncoe	....
eidz	....
edoc	....

Las matemáticas.
Write the answer in words.

1 + 1 =	dos
2 + 3 =	cinco
6 + 4 =	....
10 + 2 =	....
5 + 5 =	....
6 − 5 =	....
4 − 2 =	....
12 − 6 =	....
10 − 5 =	....
8 − 6 =	....

© Nicolette Hannam, Michelle Williams and Brilliant Publications Limited. Buena Idea.

Los números

Sentence building

Ask a question
¿Cuántos años tienes?
How old are you?

Tengo diez años.
I am ten years old.

Play a game
¿En qué número pienso?
What number am I thinking of?

¿Es el número siete?
Is it number seven?

No, más arriba.
No, higher.

No, más bajo.
No, lower.

Sí, buena respuesta.
Yes, good answer.

Count items in the room
¿Cuántos niños hay?
How many children are there?

¿Cuántas sillas hay?
How many chairs are there?

Hay ...
There are ...

Los días

Key vocabulary

lunes	Monday
martes	Tuesday
miércoles	Wednesday
jueves	Thursday
viernes	Friday
sábado	Saturday
domingo	Sunday

¿Qué día es?
What day is it?

¿Cuál es la fecha de hoy?
What's today's date?

¡Es lunes!
It's Monday!

Los días ✂ Matching cards

lunes	**Monday**
martes	**Tuesday**
miércoles	**Wednesday**
jueves	**Thursday**
viernes	**Friday**
sábado	**Saturday**
domingo	**Sunday**

Los días

Activity sheet

Nombre: .... Fecha: ....

I know the days of the week in Spanish.
Write each day of the week carefully and then draw a picture to show what you may do on that day.

lunes	
martes	
miércoles	
jueves	
viernes	
sábado	
domingo	

Adicional

What do Spanish children do on each day of the week? How does it compare to your week?

Los días Puzzle page

Busca las palabras en la sopa de letras.
Search for the words in the grid.

lunes
martes
miércoles
jueves
viernes
sábado
domingo
día

```
z  j  u  e  v  e  s  p  z  l
f  d  k  g  i  b  j  f  k  u
m  a  r  t  e  s  s  g  j  n
g  f  v  h  r  k  d  í  a  e
d  o  m  i  n  g  o  v  d  s
p  f  h  v  e  s  y  p  j  z
j  p  k  g  s  á  b  a  d  o
s  m  i  é  r  c  o  l  e  s
```

Descifra los anagramas.
Solve the anagrams.

neusl   *lunes*
leocsimér   ....
trmase   ....
moginod   ....
jvseeu   ....
dabosá   ....
nrveise   ....

¿Qué día es?
What day is it?

_ _ _ e _   *lunes*
_ _ _ r _ _ _ _
_ _ m _ _ _ _
_ _ e _ _ _
_ _ _ r _ _ _

14

Los días — Sentence building

Ask a question
¿Qué día es?   What day is it today?
¡Es lunes!   It's Monday!

¿Cuál es la fecha de hoy?   What is today's date?
Es lunes, el 4 de mayo.   It's Monday 4th May.

Add a preference
¿Cuál es tu día preferido?   What is your favourite day?

♥   *Prefiero el sábado.*   I like Saturday best.

   *Odio el lunes.*   I hate Mondays.

Sing a song
Reinforce vocabulary by singing a song such as 'Días' from *¡Vamos a Cantar!*

Los meses

Key vocabulary

enero	January
febrero	February
marzo	March
abril	April
mayo	May
junio	June
julio	July
agosto	August
septiembre	September
octubre	October
noviembre	November
diciembre	December

¿Cuál es la fecha de tu cumpleaños?
When is your birthday?

¡Mi cumpleaños es el diez de enero!
My birthday is on the 10th of January!

¿Cuál es la fecha de hoy?
What is today's date?

Es lunes, el 23 de junio.
It's Monday, 23rd June.

Los meses ✂ Matching cards

enero	January
febrero	February
marzo	March
abril	April
mayo	May
junio	June

Los meses ✂ Matching cards

julio	July
agosto	August
septiembre	September
octubre	October
noviembre	November
diciembre	December

Los meses — Activity sheet

Nombre: .... *Fecha:* ....

I know the months of the year in Spanish.

Carefully write the months of the year in Spanish. Draw a symbol for an event in each month. For example, a rabbit for Easter.

enero

Adicional

¿Cuál es la fecha de tu cumpleaños?
What day is your birthday?

Los meses

Puzzle page

Busca las palabras en la sopa de letras.
Search for the words in the grid.

enero	f	d	i	c	i	e	m	b	r	e
febrero	b	e	m	a	r	z	o	b	x	o
marzo	x	n	a	b	x	j	f	j	f	c
abril	j	e	y	r	m	u	m	u	e	t
mayo	a	r	o	i	b	n	j	l	b	u
junio	g	o	f	l	x	i	f	i	r	b
julio	o	b	m	f	j	o	x	o	e	r
agosto	s	e	p	t	i	e	m	b	r	e
septiembre	t	x	b	d	b	j	d	x	o	f
octubre	o	n	o	v	i	e	m	b	r	e
noviembre										
diciembre										

Descifra los anagramas.
Solve the anagrams.

renoe   *enero*
errebfo   ....
ymoa   ....
rebciidme   ....
tepsmiereb   ....
ozmra   ....
ljiou   ....
rliba   ....
ijuon   ....
sotaog   ....
mievonreb   ....
utcorbe   ....

¿Qué mes es?
What month is it?

_ _ _ r _   *enero*
_ _ r _ _
_ g _ _ _ _
_ _ b r _ _ _
_ _ v _ _ _ _ _ _

Los meses — Sentence building

Ask a question
¿Cuál es la fecha de tu cumpleaños?   What day is your birthday?
¡Mi cumpleaños es el diez de enero!   My birthday is on the 10th of January.

Add a preference
¿Cuál es tu mes preferido?   Which is your favourite month?

   Prefiero mayo.   My favourite is May.

   Odio enero.   I hate January.

Add the seasons
(en) primavera   (in) spring
(en) verano   (in) summer
(en) otoño   (in) autumn
(en) invierno   (in) winter

Enero es en invierno.   January is in winter.

Mayo es en primavera.   May is in spring.

Sing a song
Reinforce vocabulary by singing a song such as 'El año' from ¡Vamos a Cantar!

Mi familia

Key vocabulary

mi padre	my father
mi madre	my mother
mi padrastro	my step-dad
mi madrastra	my step-mum
mi hermano	my brother
mi hermana	my sister
mi abuelo	my grandad
mi abuela	my grandma
mi tío	my uncle
mi tía	my aunt
mi primo	my cousin (boy)
mi prima	my cousin (girl)

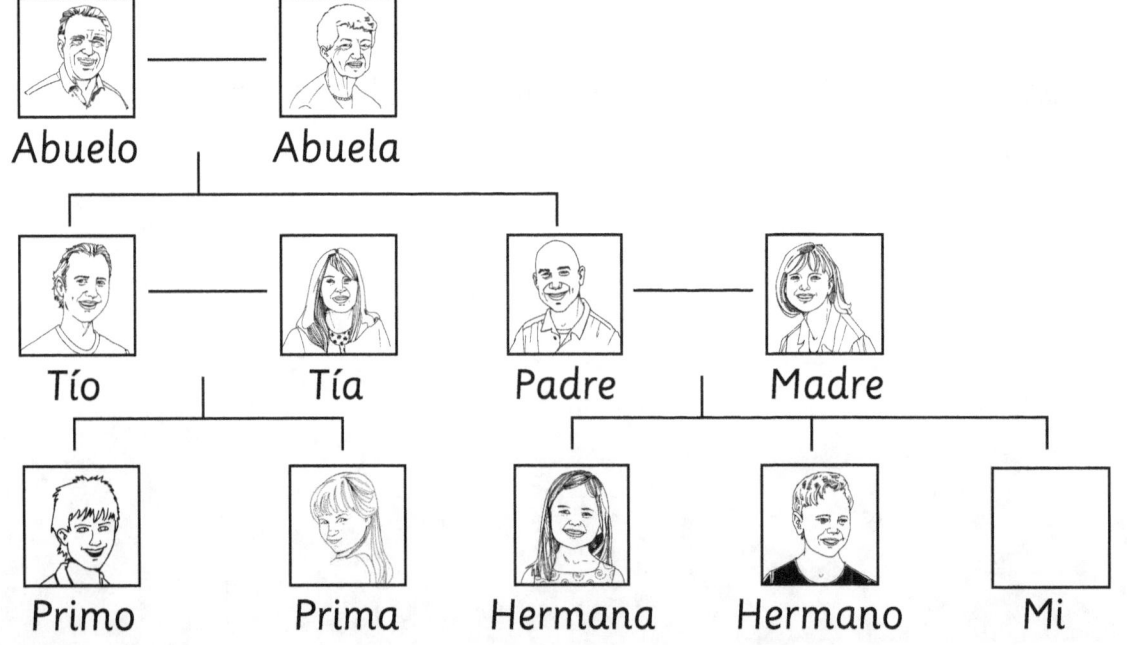

Mi familia ✂ Matching cards

padre	father
madre	mother
hermano	brother
hermana	sister
abuelo	grandad
abuela	grandma
tía	aunt
tío	uncle

Mi familia

✂ Picture cards

padre	
madre	
hermano	
hermana	
abuelo	
abuela	
tía	
tío	

Mi familia

Activity sheet

Nombre: .... Fecha: ....

I know the names of family members in Spanish.

Draw yourself in the centre of this sheet and label it with *Mi* (me). Then add your immediate family and label them. For example: *Mi hermana, Rebecca.*

Adicional

¿Cuántas personas hay en tu casa?

How many people live with you?

Mi familia
Puzzle page

Busca las palabras en la sopa de letras.
Search for the words in the grid.

padre	h	e	r	m	a	n	a	x	d	h
madre	p	a	d	r	a	s	t	r	o	e
padrastro	m	a	d	r	a	s	t	r	a	r
madrastra	t	d	a	b	u	e	l	a	d	m
hermano	í	p	a	d	r	e	j	x	l	a
hermana	a	r	z	l	o	u	q	w	o	n
abuelo	d	i	x	w	a	b	u	e	l	o
abuela	t	m	m	l	z	m	d	u	q	l
tío	í	o	j	z	p	r	i	m	a	x
tía	o	x	m	a	d	r	e	x	d	j
primo									
prima									

Descifra los anagramas.
Solve the anagrams.

im derap	mi padre
mi damre	....
im rhenmoa	....
mi hrenaam	....
mi íta	....
im oít	....
im olebau	....
mi balaeu	....

¿Quién es?
Who is it?

_ i / _ e _ _ a _ _   mi hermana
_ _ / p _ _ _ _
m _ / _ b _ _ _ a
_ i / _ _ a
m _ / _ _ o

26

Mi familia Sentence building

Add, 'en mi familia, hay ...'
En mi familia, hay mi padre, mi madre, mi hermana y yo.
In my family there is my father, my mother, my sister and me.

Add a name
Mi padre se llama George.   My father's name is George.
Mi madre se llama Mary.   My mother's name is Mary.

Add an age
Mi padre tiene 30 años.   My father is 30 years old.
Mi hermana tiene 6 años.   My sister is 6 years old.

Add a simple description
Mi padre es grande/de talla media/pequeño.
My father is tall/medium height/small.
Mi madre es grande/de talla media/pequeña.
My mother is tall/medium height/small.

Add a characteristic
Mi hermano es gracioso.   My brother is funny.
Mi hermana es habladora.   My sister is a chatterbox.

More characteristics

English	Masculine	Feminine
nice	*agradable*	*agradable*
chatty	*hablador*	*habladora*
funny	*gracioso*	*graciosa*
kind	*simpático*	*simpática*
lazy	*perezoso*	*perezosa*
fun	*divertido*	*divertida*

Sing a song
Reinforce vocabulary by singing a song such as 'Mi familia' from *¡Vamos a Cantar!*

Los colores

Key vocabulary

rojo	red
azul	blue
verde	green
amarillo	yellow
naranja	orange
marrón	brown
purpúreo	purple
rosa	pink
negro	black
blanco	white
oro	gold
plata	silver
gris	grey

¿Cuál es tu color preferido?
What is your favourite colour?
Mi color preferido es ...
My favourite colour is ...

Los colores ✂ Matching cards

rojo	red
azul	blue
naranja	orange
amarillo	yellow
verde	green
gris	grey

Los colores ✂ Matching cards

rosa	**pink**
purpúreo	**purple**
negro	**black**
blanco	**white**
oro	**gold**
plata	**silver**

Los colores ✂ Matching cards

¡Colorea las tarjetas!
Colour the cards!

rojo	
azul	
naranja	
amarillo	
verde	
rosa	

Los colores

Matching cards

¡Colorea las tarjetas!
Colour the cards!

purpúreo	
negro	
blanco	
oro	
plata	
gris	

Los colores Activity sheet

Nombre: .... Fecha: ....

I know the colours in Spanish.
Use the vocabulary box below to help you to draw some shapes. Then colour them the right colour.

un cuadrado rojo   *un círculo amarillo*   *un rectángulo azul*

un triángulo verde   *un diamante blanco*   *un rombo negro*

un cuadrado marrón   *un círculo rosa*   *un triángulo purpúreo*

un cuadrado	a square	☐	*un círculo*	a circle ○
un rectángulo	a rectangle	▭	*un triángulo*	a triangle △
un diamante	a diamond	◇	*un rombo*	a rhombus

Los colores

Puzzle page

Busca las palabras en la sopa de letras.
Search for the words in the grid.

rojo
azul
verde
amarillo
naranja
marrón
rosa
negro
blanco
oro
plata
gris

m	x	v	e	r	d	e	m	r	p
p	l	a	t	a	x	o	a	o	n
u	p	s	g	r	i	s	x	j	a
r	x	m	b	l	a	n	c	o	r
p	s	r	a	p	l	p	l	c	a
u	d	o	p	m	a	r	r	ó	n
r	o	s	o	d	p	m	p	l	j
a	m	a	r	i	l	l	o	x	a
s	a	z	u	l	a	m	r	d	o
d	o	s	n	e	g	r	o	m	d

Descifra los anagramas.
Solve the anagrams.

joor   rojo
saro   ....
zalu   ....
aarnnaj   ....

ornge   ....
clabno   ....
edrev   ....
rórman   ....

¿De qué colores?
What colour is made?

rojo + blanco =   rosa
rojo + amarillo = ...
azul + amarillo = ...
blanco + negro = ...
azul + rojo = ...

Une los dibujos con las palabras.
Match the words and pictures.

A   B   C

rojo   ....
verde   ....
azul   ....

Los colores Sentence building

Add a question and a preference
¿Cuál es tu color preferido?   What is your favourite colour?

Mi color preferido es azul.   My favourite colour is blue.

Add a noun
*Tengo una camiseta **negra**.*   I have a **black** t-shirt.
*Tengo un jersey **verde**.*   I have a **green** jumper.
*Tengo un vestido **azul**.*   I have a **blue** dress.

Remember, colours in Spanish follow the noun!

Sing a song
Reinforce vocabulary by singing a song such as 'El mundo es un arco iris' from *¡Vamos a Cantar!*

Los animales

	Key vocabulary
un perro	a dog
un gato	a cat
un conejo	a rabbit
un hámster	a hamster
un ratón	a mouse
un pájaro	a bird
un pez	a fish
un conejillo de Indias	a guinea pig

¿Tienes un animal?
Do you have a pet?

Tengo un gato y un perro.
I have a cat and a dog.

No, no tengo animales.
No, I haven't got any pets.

Los animales Matching cards

un perro	a dog
un gato	a cat
un conejo	a rabbit
un pájaro	a bird
un pez	a fish
un ratón	a mouse
un conejillo de Indias	a guinea pig
un hámster	a hamster

Los animales — Picture cards

un perro	
un gato	
un conejo	
un pájaro	
un pez	
un conejillo de Indias	
un hámster	

Los animales   Activity sheet

Nombre: ....   *Fecha:* ....

I know the names of animals in Spanish.

Draw the animals described below.
Make sure you use the right colour!

un perro azul   un gato verde   un ratón rosa

un pájaro blanco   un conejo amarillo   un hámster rojo

un pez marrón   un conejillo de Indias negro

Adicional

¿Tienes un animal?
Do you have a pet?

Los animales — Puzzle page

Busca las palabras en la sopa de letras.
Search for the words in the grid.

perro
gato
conejo
hámster
ratón
pájaro
pez

```
c d h á m s t e r h
o t h l p á j a r o
n g b d e t h l a t
e l a l r o x o t d
j o z t r x d x ó z
o t h z o p e z n h
```

Descifra los anagramas.
Solve the anagrams.

tgao	*gato*
ojenoc	....
tónar	....
japorá	....
pze	....
rrpoe	....
stráhme	....

Adivina el animal.
Guess the animal.

_ _ / c _ _ _ _ _
u _ / _ a _ _ n
_ _ / _ _ _ r o
_ _ / _ _ j _ _ o
_ _ / _ _ _

¿Quién es?
Who am I?

I bark. ....
I squeak. ....
I miaow. ....
I like carrots. ....

Une los dibujos con las palabras.
Match the words and pictures.

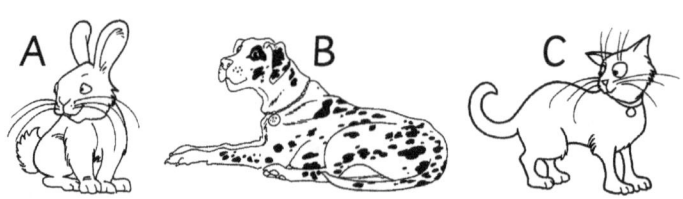

A   B   C

un *gato* ....
un *conejo* ....
un *perro* ....

Los animales — Sentence building

Ask a question
¿Tienes un animal?   Do you have a pet?

Use 'Tengo …' or 'No, no tengo …'
Sí, tengo un gato/un perro.   Yes, I have a cat/a dog.
No, no tengo animales.   No, I don't have a pet.

Add the connective 'y'
*Tengo un perro **y** un gato.*   I have a dog and a cat.

Add a name
Tengo un gato, 'Fluff'.   I have a cat, 'Fluff'.
*Tengo un perro **que se llama** 'Patch'.*   I have dog called 'Patch'.

Add a colour
Remember colours in Spanish follow the noun!
*Tengo un gato **gris**.*   I have a grey cat.
*Tengo un perro **marrón**.*   I have a brown dog.
*Tengo un ratón **gris**.*   I have a grey mouse.

Add an opinion
*Me gusta(n) **mi** perro/**mi** ratón/**mis** peces.*
I like my dog/my mouse/my fish.

*Me encanta(n) **mi** conejo/**mi** ratón/**mis** gatos.*
I love my rabbit/my mouse/my cats.

Sing a song
Reinforce vocabulary by singing a song such as 'Animales' from *¡Vamos a Cantar!*

Nicolette Hannam, Michelle Williams and Brilliant Publications Limited. Buena Idea.

En el aula — Key vocabulary

una puerta	a door
una ventana	a window
una mesa	a table
una silla	a chair
un ordenador	a computer
una pizarra	a board
un profesor	a teacher
un cuaderno	an exercise book
un libro	a text book
mi estuche	my pencil case
una regla	a ruler
una goma	an eraser
un lápiz	a pencil
un sacapuntas	a pencil sharpener
un bolígrafo	a pen
unas tijeras	scissors
unos rotuladores	felt tips

En el aula, hay ...
In the classroom, there is ...

En el aula ✂ Matching cards

una mesa	**a table**
una silla	**a chair**
un libro	**a book**
un lápiz	**a pencil**
un bolígrafo	**a pen**
una regla	**a ruler**

En el aula ✂ Matching cards

una goma	an eraser
unos rotuladores	a felt tip
una puerta	a door
mi estuche	my pencil case
una ventana	a window
unas tijeras	scissors

En el aula

✂ Picture cards

una mesa	
una silla	
un libro	
un lápiz	
un bolígrafo	
una regla	

En el aula   ✂ Picture cards

una goma	
unos rotuladores	
una puerta	
mi estuche	
una ventana	
unas tijeras	

En el aula

Activity sheet

Nombre: .... Fecha: ....

I know the names of objects in the classroom in Spanish.

Unscramble these words and write them correctly. Then draw a picture to match each word.

una geral
....

una aannevt
....

una atreup
....

mi heecuts
....

un ducareno
....

un zpilá
....

una llsia
....

saun srajite
....

aun moga
....

Adicional

Now choose two words to scramble yourself. Write them here.

En el aula

Puzzle page

Busca las palabras en la sopa de letras.
Search for the words in the grid.

puerta
ventana
mesa
silla
ordenador
pizarra
libro
estuche
regla
goma
sacapuntas
tijeras

```
x o r d e n a d o r
k p u p i t m e s a
k i x m r e g l a x
e z r g o m a j i m
s a c a p u n t a s
t r x i p u r i n i
u r i r x n e j x l
c a r m l i b r o l
h t i j e r a s t a
e i x v e n t a n a
```

Descifra los anagramas.
Solve the anagrams.

reducano   cuaderno
rlboi   ....
ílobgaorf   ....
taruep   ....
amgo   ....
allis   ....
drolauortse   ....

¿Qué es?
What am I?

_ _ / l _ _ _ _
u _ _ / _ u e _ _ _
_ n / c _ _ _ _ _ _ _
_ _ _ / _ e n _ _ _ _
u _ _ / _ _ g _ _

¿Qué es?
What am I?

You write with me.   ....
You write in me.   ....
You sit on me.   ....
I am different colours. ....
I am sharp.   ....

Une los dibujos con las palabras.
Match the words and pictures.

A   B   C
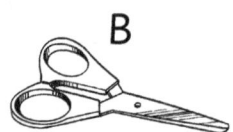   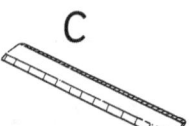

una regla   ....
un lápiz   ....
unas tijeras   ....

En el aula

Sentence building

Ask questions
¿Qué tienes en tu aula?
What have you got in your classroom?

¿Qué tienes en tu bolsa?
What have you got in your bag?

Use, 'en mi aula, hay...'
En mi aula, hay *una puerta, un ordenador ...*
In my classroom there is a door, a computer ...
or
En mi bolsa, hay *un libro, mi estuche y una regla.*
In my bag, there is a book, my pencil case and a ruler.

Reinforce numbers
¿Cuántas puertas hay en el aula?
How many doors are there in the classroom?

Sing a song
Reinforce vocabulary by singing a song such as 'Vamos a movernos' from *¡Vamos a Cantar!*

Las asignaturas

Key vocabulary

inglés	English
español	Spanish
matemáticas	maths
biología	science
historia	history
geografía	geography
educación física	PE
dibujo	art
música	music
tecnología	technology

¿Cuál es tu asignatura preferida?
What is your favourite subject?
Me gusta(n) ...   I like ...
Me encanta(n) ...   I love ...
No me gusta(n) ... I don't like ...
Odio ...   I hate ...

Las asignaturas  Matching cards

español	Spanish
inglés	English
biología	science
matemáticas	maths
historia	history
geografía	geography

Las asignaturas — Matching cards

educación física	**PE**
dibujo	art
tecnología	technology
música	music
me gusta(n) ...	I like ...
no me gusta(n) ...	I don't like ...

Las asignaturas

Activity sheet

Nombre: .... Fecha: ....

I know the names of school subjects in Spanish.
Write each of the school subjects from the vocabulary box below in the correct column in the table to show how much you like each one.

Me encanta(n) …	Me gusta(n) …	No me gusta(n) …	Odio …

inglés	English	*español*	Spanish
matemáticas	maths	*biología*	science
historia	history	*geografía*	geography
educación física	PE	*dibujo*	art
música	music	*tecnología*	technology

Adicional

¿Cuál es tu asignatura preferida?
Which is your favourite subject?

Las asignaturas — Puzzle page

Busca las palabras en la sopa de letras.
Search for the words in the grid.

inglés
español
matemáticas
biología
historia
geografía
dibujo
música
tecnología

```
v t e c n o l o g í a
i h i s t o r i a v x
n x b l p o l x o y b
g e o g r a f í a x v
l m x m y k ñ w k o w
é l w b i o l o g í a
s v y g o x k g l w o
k w d i b u j o y g x
l x g o m ú s i c a w
m a t e m á t i c a s
```

Descifra los anagramas.
Solve the anagrams.

sléngi	inglés
gooíalbi	....
iitshaor	....
ojbdui	....
camisú	....
rggoeaaíf	....
sacitammáte	....

¿Qué es?
Which subject?

¡Hola!	español
Bang the drum	....
Paints	....
Times table	....
Throw a ball	....

Une los dibujos con las palabras.
Match the words and pictures.

A  B  C 9×3 =27

geografía ....
educación física ....
matemáticas ....

Las asignaturas — Sentence building

Add a preference
¿Cuál es tu asignatura preferida? — What is your favourite subject?
Mi asignatura preferida es el español. — My favourite subject is Spanish.

Add an opinion

 *Me gusta el español.* — I like Spanish.

 *Me encanta la educación física.* — I love sport.

 No me gusta el dibujo. — I don't like art.

 *Odio la geografía.* — I hate geography.

Extend the opinion

Es interesante.	It's interesting.
Es fácil.	It's easy.
Es aburrido.	It's boring.
Es difícil.	It's difficult.

La comida

Key vocabulary

una pizza	a pizza
un perrito caliente	a hot-dog
una hamburguesa	a hamburger
una tortilla	an omelette
las patatas fritas	chips
el pollo	chicken
el queso	cheese
las legumbres	vegetables
un bocadillo	a sandwich
un pastel	a cake
un helado	an ice-cream
caramelos	sweets
un zumo de naranja	an orange juice
una cola	a cola
una limonada	a lemonade
un café	a coffee
un té	a tea
quisiera ...	I would like ...
por favor	please
gracias	thank you

La comida

una pizza	pizza
las patatas fritas	chips
el pollo	chicken
las legumbres	vegetables
el queso	cheese
un pastel	cake

La comida ✂ Matching cards

un té	a tea
una cola	a cola
un café	a coffee
caramelos	sweets
un helado	an ice-cream
quisiera ...	I would like ...

La comida

Picture cards

una pizza	
las patatas fritas	
el pollo	
las legumbres	
el queso	
un pastel	

La comida ✂ Picture cards

un té	
una cola	
un café	
caramelos	
un helado	
una hamburguesa	

La comida   Activity sheet

Nombre: .... *Fecha:* ....

I know the names of some food and drinks in Spanish.
Draw and label a meal below, including main meal, dessert and a drink. Choose from the vocabulary in the box below.

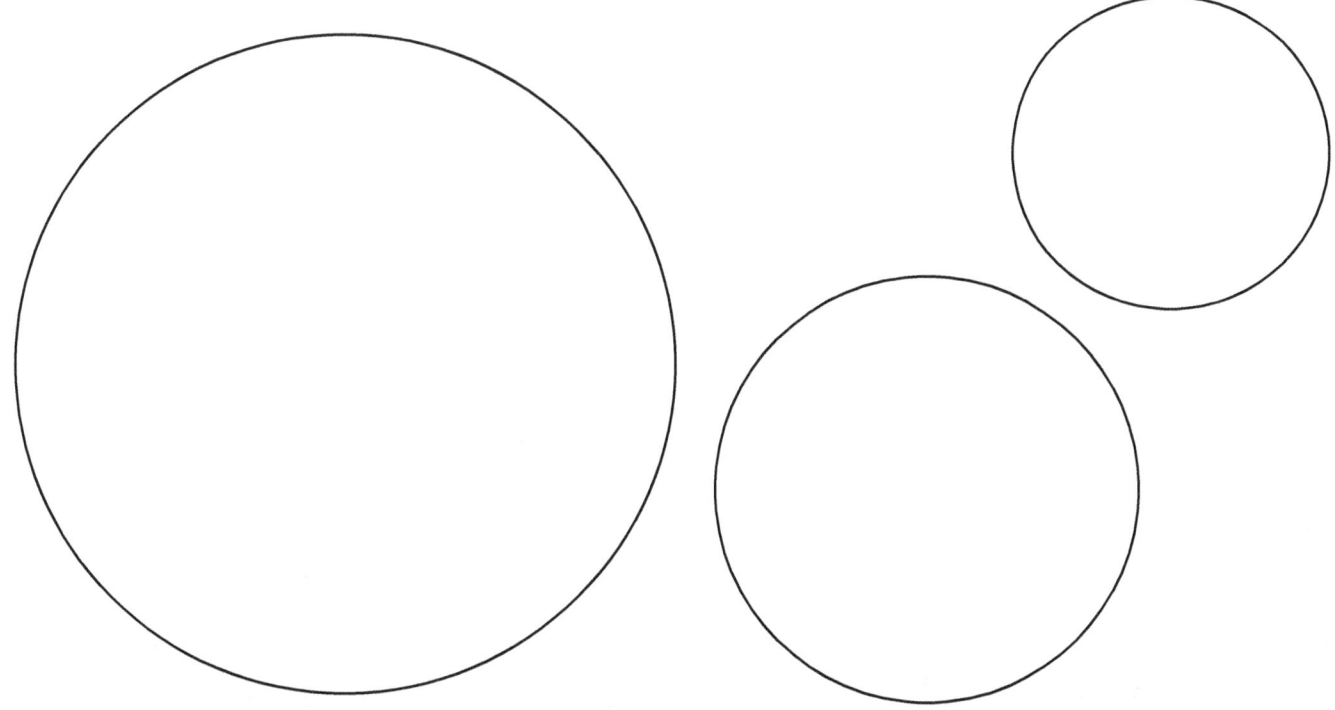

una pizza	a pizza	*un perrito caliente*	a hot-dog
una hamburguesa	a hamburger	*una tortilla*	an omelette
las patatas fritas	chips	*el pollo*	chicken
el queso	cheese	*las legumbres*	vegetables
un bocadillo	a sandwich	*un pastel*	a cake
un helado	an ice-cream	*caramelos*	sweets
un zumo de naranja	an orange juice	*una cola*	a cola
un café	a coffee	*un té*	a tea

Adicional

¿Qué te gusta comer?
What do you like to eat?

La comida   Puzzle page

Busca las palabras en la sopa de letras.
Search for the words in the grid.

pizza
tortilla
pollo
queso
legumbres
bocadillo
pastel
helado
caramelos
limonada
café
gracias

b	c	a	r	a	m	e	l	o	s
o	x	a	v	g	h	u	i	p	k
c	g	h	f	q	x	l	m	i	q
a	k	q	h	é	x	c	o	z	u
d	p	o	l	l	o	e	n	z	e
i	a	g	q	k	h	s	a	a	s
l	s	v	h	e	l	a	d	o	o
l	t	g	r	a	c	i	a	s	v
o	e	t	o	r	t	i	l	l	a
x	l	e	g	u	m	b	r	e	s

Descifra los anagramas.
Solve the anagrams.

zizap   *pizza*
llopo   ....
gmuleresb   ....
soeuq   ....
tselpa   ....
écaf   ....
lloidcaob   ....

Une los dibujos con las palabras.
Match the words and pictures.

A    B    C

el pollo   ....
una pizza   ....
una cola   ....

Completa la lista.
Complete the list.

Tapas saladas (savoury snacks)	Tapas dulces (sweet snacks)	Bebidas (drinks)
las patatas fritas	*pastel*	*café*

La comida — Sentence building

Make up a café dialogue
Useful vocabulary

A ***Buenos días Señor/Señorita.***
Hello Sir/Madam.
¿Qué desea usted?
What would you like?

B ***Quisiera una pizza y patatas fritas por favor.***
I'd like a pizza and chips please.

A ***¿Algo más?***
Anything else?

B ***Quisiera un zumo de naranja por favor.***
An orange juice please.
Es delicioso.
It's delicious.
La cuenta por favor.
The bill please.

A ***Aquí tiene, son 8 euros. Gracias.***
Here you are, that's 8 euros, thank you.

B ***Gracias. Adiós.***
Thank you. Goodbye.

Add an opinion

   ***Me gusta el pollo.***   I like chicken.

   ***Me encantan los caramelos.***   I love sweets.

   No me gustan las legumbres.   I don't like vegetables.

   ***Odio el queso.***   I hate cheese.

Sing a song
Reinforce vocabulary by singing a song such as 'No me gustan. No' from *¡Vamos a Cantar!*

¿Qué tiempo hace?

Key vocabulary

llueve	**it's raining**
nieva	**it's snowing**
hace sol	**it's sunny**
hace viento	**it's windy**
hay niebla	**it's foggy**
hay tormentas	**it's stormy**
hace frío	**it's cold**
hace calor	**it's hot**

hoy	today
mañana	tomorrow

en Barcelona ...	in Barcelona
en Leeds ...	in Leeds
en el norte	in the North
en el sur	in the South
en el este	in the East
en el oeste	in the West

¿Qué tiempo hace? ✂ Matching cards

llueve	it's raining
nieva	it's snowing
hace frío	it's cold
hace calor	it's hot
hace viento	it's windy
hace sol	it's sunny
hay tormentas	it's stormy
hay niebla	it's foggy

¿Qué tiempo hace? ✂ Picture cards

llueve	
nieva	
hace frío	
hace calor	
hace viento	
hace sol	
hay tormentas	
hay niebla	

¿Qué tiempo hace?   Activity sheet

Nombre: ....   Fecha: ....

I can describe the weather in Spanish.

Draw lines to match up the English weather phrase to the correct Spanish phrase. Then draw a picture to match each Spanish phrase.

It is stormy	*Llueve*	
It is windy	*Nieva*	
It is raining	*Hace sol*	
It is sunny	*Hace viento*	
It is snowing	*Hay tormenta*	

Adicional

¿Qué tiempo hace?

What's the weather like today?

¿Qué tiempo hace? Puzzle page

Busca las palabras en la sepa de letras.
Search for the words in the grid.

w	t	o	r	m	e	n	t	a	s
n	i	e	v	a	x	s	w	l	n
l	s	o	l	ñ	z	n	t	o	i
l	u	n	c	a	l	o	r	e	e
u	r	z	t	n	q	r	w	s	b
e	x	w	q	a	j	t	u	t	l
v	i	e	n	t	o	e	l	e	a
e	f	r	í	o	x	t	h	o	y

llueve
nieva
sol
viento
niebla
tormentas
frío
calor
hoy
mañana
norte
sur
este
oeste

Descifra los anagramas.
Solve the anagrams.

eevull   llueve
vaien   ....
ceha lorca   ....
ache eintov   ....
hcea oífr   ....
ecah los   ....

Une los dibujos con las palabras.
Match the words and pictures.

A   B   C

nieva   ....
llueve   ....
hace sol   ....

¿Qué tiempo hace? Sentence building

Add a town
En Mirfield, hace sol.   In Mirfield, it's hot.
En Leeds, hace frío.   In Leeds, it's cold.

Add a country
En España, hace calor.   In Spain, it's sunny.
En Inglaterra, hay tormentas.   In England, it's stormy.

Use a weather map and make a forecast
En el norte, nieva.   In the North, it's snowing.
En el sur, hay niebla.   In the South, it's foggy.
En el este, hace frío.   In the East, it's cold.
En el oeste, hay tormentas.   In the West, it's stormy.

Add the seasons
En primavera, hace buen tiempo.   In the spring, it's nice weather.
En verano …   In the summer …
En otoño …   In the autumn …
En invierno …   In the winter …

Sing a song
Reinforce vocabulary by singing a song such as 'El año' from *¡Vamos a Cantar!*

El cuerpo

Key vocabulary

la cara	face
la nariz	nose
la cabeza	head
la boca	mouth
los ojos	eyes
las orejas	ears
el pelo	hair
los hombros	shoulders
el brazo	arm
la mano	hand
el estómago	stomach
la espalda	back
la pierna	leg
la rodilla	knee
el pie	foot

Tengo dolor de cabeza.
I've got a headache.
Tengo dolor de espalda.
I've got backache.
Tengo dolor de orejas.
I've got earache.

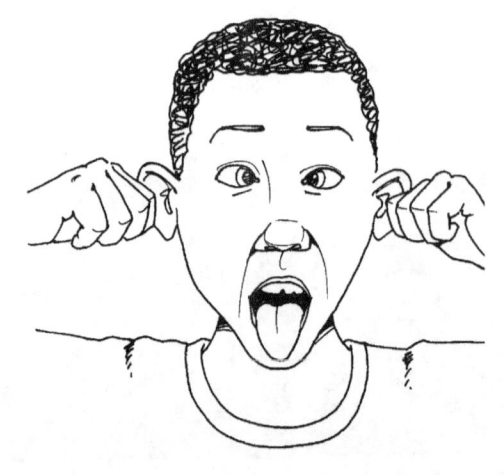

El cuerpo ✂ Matching cards

los ojos	eyes
la cabeza	head
las orejas	ears
la boca	mouth
la mano	hand
la pierna	leg

El cuerpo ✂ Matching cards

el brazo	arm
el estómago	stomach
la espalda	back
la rodilla	knee
el pie	foot
el pelo	hair

El cuerpo

✂ Picture cards

los ojos	
la cara	
las orejas	
la boca	
la mano	
la pierna	

El cuerpo

✂ Picture cards

el brazo	
el estómago	
la espalda	
la rodilla	
el pie	
el pelo	

El cuerpo

Activity sheet

Nombre: .... Fecha: ....

I know the parts of the body in Spanish.

Draw the monster that is described in the box below:

> Mi monstruo tiene dos cabezas,
> Cuatro brazos y ocho orejas.
> Mi monstruo tiene cuatro manos,
> Tres piernas y tres pies.
> Mi monstruo tiene una boca,
> Siete ojos y dos narices.

Adicional

Which colours have you used on your monster? Can you list them, in Spanish?

El cuerpo

Puzzle page

Busca las palabras en la sopa de letras.
Search for the words in the grid.

cara
nariz
cabeza
boca
ojos
orejas
pelo
hombro
brazo
mano
estómago
pierna
rodilla

d	q	r	o	d	i	l	l	a	x
p	i	e	r	n	a	x	o	z	d
e	q	o	l	o	r	e	j	a	s
l	c	x	z	q	n	q	m	h	o
o	a	a	m	d	a	o	j	o	s
z	r	k	b	h	r	k	z	m	z
x	a	q	h	e	i	x	q	b	m
m	x	o	z	l	z	h	d	r	a
o	e	s	t	ó	m	a	g	o	n
b	o	c	a	x	b	r	a	z	o

Descifra los anagramas.
Solve the anagrams.

al zbcaae   la cabeza
la nmao   ....
le zobar   ....
la peslaad   ....
al cboa   ....
ols joos   ....
al ienrap   ....

Escribe las palabras adecuandos.
Write labels.

La cabeza

76

El cuerpo — Sentence building

Play a game using *'toca ...'*
Toca la nariz. Touch your nose.
Toca los ojos. Touch your eyes.

Reinforce numbers using *'tengo'* for I have
Tengo dos piernas. I have two legs.

Tengo una boca. I have one mouth.

Introduce negatives
No tengo cuatro rodillas. I have not got four knees.

Introduce illness
Tengo dolor de cabeza. I have a headache.
Tengo dolor de espalda. I have backache.
Tengo dolor de orejas. I have earache.

Sing a song
Reinforce vocabulary by singing a song such as 'Ay, ay, ay' from *¡Vamos a Cantar!*

Sing 'Head, shoulders, knees and toes' in Spanish (literally in Spanish you sing 'Head, shoulders, knees and feet'):

Cabeza, hombros, rodillas, pies, rodillas, pies
Cabeza, hombros, rodillas, pies, rodillas, pies

Ojos, orejas, boca, nariz,
Cabeza, hombros, rodillas, pies, rodillas, pies.

Mis pasatiempos

Key vocabulary

Juego al fútbol	I play football
Juego al rugby	I play rugby
Juego al tenis	I play tennis
Hago el monopatín	I go skateboarding
Voy en bici	I ride my bike
Voy de compras	I go shopping
Monto a caballo	I go horse riding
Nado	I swim
Bailo	I dance
Escucho música	I listen to music
Veo la tele	I watch TV
Voy al cine	I go to the cinema

con mis amigos	with my friends
el fin de semana	at the weekend

Mis pasatiempos ✂ Matching cards

Juego al fútbol	I play football
Voy en bici	I ride my bike
Nado	I swim
Voy de compras	I go shopping
Voy al cine	I go to the cinema
Veo la tele	I watch TV

Mis pasatiempos ✂ Matching cards

Escucho música	**I listen to music**
Bailo	**I go dancing**
Juego al tenis	**I play tennis**
Juego al rugby	**I play rugby**
Hago el monopatín	**I go skateboarding**
Monto a caballo	**I go horse riding**

Mis pasatiempos ✂ Picture cards

Juego al fútbol	
Voy en bici	
Nado	
Voy de compras	
Voy al cine	
Veo la tele	

Mis pasatiempos ✂ Picture cards

Escucho música	
Bailo	
Juego al tenis	
Juego al rugby	
Hago el monopatín	
Voy a caballo	

Mis pasatiempos — Activity sheet

Nombre: .... Fecha: ....

I can describe my hobbies in Spanish.

Draw yourself below. Then choose at least four phrases from the vocabulary box to describe your hobbies. Copy them neatly around your picture. Illustrate your ideas.

Juego al fútbol	I play football	*Juego al rugby*	I play rugby
Juego al tenis	I play tennis	*Hago el monopatín*	I go skateboarding
Voy en bici	I ride my bike	*Voy de compras*	I go shopping
Monto a caballo	I horse ride	*Nado*	I swim
Bailo	I dance	*Veo la tele*	I watch TV
Voy al cine	I go to the cinema	*Escucho música*	I listen to music

Adicional

¿Cuál es tu pasatiempo preferido?

What is your favourite hobby?

Mis pasatiempos — Puzzle page

Busca las palabras en la sopa de letras.
Search for the words in the grid.

rugby
tenis
equitación
natación
bailo
música
tele
cine
amigos
semana

b	l	n	a	t	a	c	i	ó	n
a	x	v	g	z	t	e	n	i	s
i	b	m	ú	s	i	c	a	g	e
l	e	g	x	p	v	b	e	l	m
o	g	r	e	a	z	l	d	z	a
e	q	u	i	t	a	c	i	ó	n
z	e	g	c	i	b	d	e	v	a
l	d	b	i	n	v	g	x	b	g
b	g	y	n	a	m	i	g	o	s
t	e	l	e	r	z	b	v	x	b

Descifra los anagramas.
Solve the anagrams.

al lotfúb   *al fútbol*
iloab   ....
yov la ince   ....
uegoj   ....
ovy ne cbii   ....
oev al leet   ....

Une los dibujos con las palabras.
Match the words and pictures.

A   B   C

Juego al tenis.   ....
Veo la tele.   ....
Monto en bici.   ....

Mis pasatiempos — Sentence building

Say when
Juego al fútbol el fin de semana.	I play football at the weekend.
Voy al cine el sábado.	I go to the cinema on Saturdays.

Say who with
Juego al fútbol con mi amigo.	I play with my friend (boy).
Juego al tenis con mi amiga.	I play with my friend (girl).
Voy en monopatín con mis amigos.	I skateboard with my friends.
Voy al cine con mi familia.	I go to the cinema with my family.

Add an opinion

 *Me gusta el fútbol.* — I like football.

 *Me encanta el baile.* — I love dancing.

 No me gusta el rugby. — I don't like rugby.

 *Odio el tenis.* — I hate tennis.

Extend the opinion
Es estupendo.	It's marvelous.
Es fenomenal.	It's great.
Es aburrido.	It's boring.

Sing a song
Reinforce vocabulary by singing a song such as 'Señorita Dinamita' from *¡Vamos a Cantar!*

La ropa

	Key vocabulary
una falda	a skirt
una chaqueta	a jacket
un vestido	a dress
una camiseta	a t-shirt
los vaqueros	jeans
un pantalón	trousers
los pantalones cortos	shorts
un jersey	a jumper
un pijama	pyjamas
las zapatillas de deporte	trainers
los zapatos	shoes

¿Qué llevas?
What are you wearing?

Llevo ...   I am wearing ...

los vaqueros **azules**   **blue** jeans
un vestido **verde**   a **green** dress

La ropa — Matching cards

llevo	I am wearing ...
los vaqueros	jeans
un pantalón	trousers
un jersey	a jumper
una camiseta	a t-shirt
los pantalones cortos	shorts

La ropa ✂ Matching cards

un pijama	pyjamas
un vestido	a dress
una chaqueta	a jacket
una falda	a skirt
las zapatillas de deporte	trainers
los zapatos	shoes

La ropa

✂ Picture cards

llevo	
los vaqueros	
un pantalón	
un jersey	
una camiseta	
los pantalones cortos	

La ropa

✂ Picture cards

un pijama	
un vestido	
una chaqueta	
una falda	
las zapatillas de deporte	
los zapatos	

La ropa

Activity sheet

Nombre: .... Fecha: ....

I can name items of clothing in Spanish.

Draw and colour the clothing described in each of the following:

una falda azul

un pantalón verde

los zapatos negros y blancos

un jersey rojo

Adicional

Now draw and describe some of your clothes, in Spanish.

La ropa

Puzzle page

Busca las palabras en la sopa de letras.
Search for the words in the grid.

falda
chaqueta
vestido
camiseta
pantalón
jersey
pijama
zapatos

f	v	p	a	n	t	a	l	ó	n
a	l	i	m	o	l	z	v	m	z
l	m	j	e	r	s	e	y	g	a
d	c	a	m	i	s	e	t	a	p
a	v	m	o	g	l	o	z	v	a
c	h	a	q	u	e	t	a	m	t
m	l	v	g	v	o	z	m	z	o
v	e	s	t	i	d	o	c	g	s

Descifra los anagramas.
Solve the anagrams.

nau flada	una falda
nu resjey	....
ols paazots	....
nu iodtsev	....
aun euathcaq	....
un maajip	....

¿Qué es?
What is it?

_ n / _ _ _ t _ _ o
_ _ a / _ a _ _ s _ _ _
_ _ / _ _ j _ _ a
_ n / _ _ _ _ e y
_ l _ _ _

Une los dibujos con las palabras.
Match the words and pictures.

A   B   C

los vaqueros ....
una falda ....
las zapatillas de deporte ....

La ropa

Sentence building

Describe what you are wearing

¿Qué llevas?	What are you wearing?
Llevo los vaqueros y una camiseta.	I'm wearing jeans and a t-shirt.

Describe your ideal uniform

Mi uniforme ideal, es un jersey y unos vaqueros.
My ideal uniform is a jumper and jeans.

Add a colour
Remember colours in Spanish follow the noun!

Tengo una camiseta **negra.**	I have a black t-shirt.
Tengo un jersey **verde.**	I have a green jumper.
Tengo una falda **azul.**	I have a blue skirt.

Sing a song

Reinforce vocabulary by singing a song such as '¿Qué hay en la tienda?' from *¡Vamos a Cantar!*

En la ciudad

Key vocabulary

la panadería	the bakery
la pastelería	the cake shop
el correos	the post office
la piscina	the swimming pool
la playa	the beach
la estación	the station
la escuela	the school
el supermercado	the supermarket
el mercado	the market
el café	the café
el cine	the cinema
el museo	the museum
el ayuntamiento	the town hall

Éste es el cine.	This is the cinema.
¿Dónde vive usted?	Where do you live?
Vivo en Leeds.	I live in Leeds.
En mi ciudad, hay …	In my town, there is …

En la ciudad ✂ Matching cards

la panadería	the bakery
la pastelería	the cake shop
la estación	the train station
el correos	the post office
el museo	the museum
el supermercado	the supermarket

En la ciudad ✂ Matching cards

el café	the café
la piscina	the swimming pool
la escuela	the school
el cine	the cinema
la playa	the beach
la ciudad	the town

En la ciudad — Picture cards

la panadería	
la pastelería	
la estación	
el correos	
el museo	
el supermercado	

En la ciudad

✂ Picture cards

el café	
la piscina	
la escuela	
el cine	
la playa	
la ciudad	

En la ciudad

Activity sheet

Nombre: .... Fecha: ....

I can name places in a town in Spanish.

For each of the buildings below, draw items that can be bought or found inside it.

| la pastelería | el mercado | la escuela |

| la piscina | el correos | el café |

Adicional

Which currency is used in Spanish shops?

En la ciudad

Puzzle page

Busca las palabras en la sopa de letras.
Search for the words in the grid.

panadería
pastelería
piscina
playa
estación
escuela
mercado
café
cine
museo

```
x  e  s  c  u  e  l  a  x  c
p  a  s  t  e  l  e  r  í  a
a  i  v  x  p  z  v  p  l  f
n  z  s  v  c  i  n  e  z  é
a  l  v  c  x  o  l  o  m  x
d  x  l  z  i  p  z  v  u  p
e  p  o  r  b  n  o  z  s  v
r  z  p  l  a  y  a  r  e  l
í  x  m  e  r  c  a  d  o  x
a  e  s  t  a  c  i  ó  n  l
```

Descifra los anagramas.
Solve the anagrams.

al daaenpíra — la panadería
la aóicnset — ....
el éfac — ....
al anicsip — ....
el enic — ....
al yaalp — ....

Une los dibujos con las palabras.
Match the words and pictures.

A   B

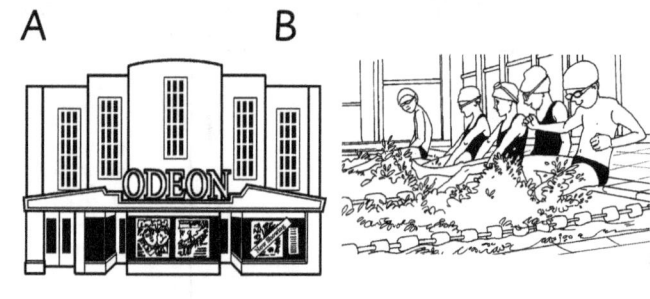

C

la piscina   ....
el café   ....
el cine   ....

¿Dónde estoy?
Where am I?

You can swim here.   la piscina
You can watch films here.   ....
You buy stamps here.   ....
You buy cakes here.   ....
You have lessons here.   ....

En la ciudad — Sentence building

Say where you live using *'vivo en ...'*
Vivo en Leeds.   I live in Leeds.

Say what there is in your town
En mi ciudad, **hay** ...   In my town **there is** a ...

Use some prepositions
El banco está **enfrente** del correos.
The bank is **opposite** the post office.

La piscina está **al lado** de la estación.
The swimming pool is **next to** the station.

La panadería está **entre** la piscina y el banco.
The bakery is **between** the pool and the bank.

El café está **enfrente** de la escuela.
The café is **in front** of the school.

El supermercado está **detrás** del banco.
The supermarket is **behind** the bank.

Sing a song
Reinforce vocabulary by singing a song such as '¿Dónde está Juanita?' from *¡Vamos a Cantar!*

Mi casa

Key vocabulary

una casa	a house
un piso	a flat
las habitaciones	the rooms
arriba	upstairs
abajo	downstairs
un salón	a lounge
una cocina	a kitchen
un comedor	a dining room
un cuarto de baño	a bathroom
un aseo	a toilet
un dormitorio	a bedroom
mi dormitorio	my bedroom
un garaje	a garage
un jardín	a garden

En mi casa, hay …   In my house there is …

Mi casa ✂ Matching cards

una casa	a house
un piso	a flat
una cocina	a kitchen
un comedor	a dining room
un cuarto de baño	a bathroom
un salón	a lounge

Mi casa   ✂ Matching cards

un dormitorio	a bedroom
un aseo	a toilet
un garaje	a garage
un jardín	a garden
arriba	upstairs
abajo	downstairs

Mi casa

✂ Picture cards

una casa	
un piso	
una cocina	
un comedor	
un cuarto de baño	
un salón	

Mi casa

✂ Picture cards

un dormitorio	
un aseo	
un garaje	
un jardín	
arriba	
abajo	

Mi casa

Activity sheet

Nombre: .... Fecha: ....

I can name the rooms in house in Spanish.
Use the space below to draw and label a typical house, using the vocabulary in the box below. You may have to draw two separate floors.

arriba	upstairs	*abajo*	downstairs
un salón	a lounge	*una cocina*	the kitchen
un comedor	the dining room	*el aseo*	the toilet
un dormitorio	the bedroom	*mi dormitorio*	my bedroom
un garaje	the garage	*un jardín*	the garden
un cuarto de baño	the bathroom		

Ideas for home: you could draw and label your dream house on large paper. Or build a 3D model.

Adicional

Can you name any types of furniture, in Spanish? You could use a dictionary to help you.

Mi casa — Puzzle page

Busca las palabras en la sopa de letras.
Search for the words in the grid.

casa
piso
habitación
arriba
abajo
salón
cocina
comedor
dormitorio
garaje
jardín

g	c	o	m	e	d	o	r	h	g
d	o	r	m	i	t	o	r	i	o
p	g	j	a	r	d	í	n	h	c
i	c	r	h	p	a	b	a	j	o
s	a	r	g	a	r	a	j	e	c
o	s	a	l	ó	n	g	p	r	i
h	a	b	i	t	a	c	i	ó	n
p	g	r	h	a	r	r	i	b	a

Descifra los anagramas.
Solve the anagrams.

im saac — mi casa
aun ccniao — ....
nu grjeaa — ....
un dínjra — ....
rrabia — ....
im mrodooiirt — ....

¿Qué sitio es …?
Which room is …?

Where you sleep — un dormitorio
Where you cook — ....
Where you play outside — ....
Where you watch tv — ....
Where you get washed — ....

Une los dibujos con las palabras.
Match the words and pictures.

A

B

C

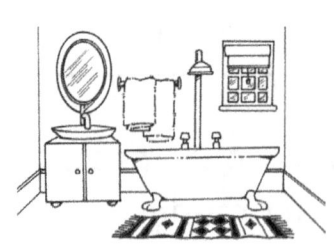

un jardín ....
mi dormitorio ....
un cuarto de baño ....

Mi casa — Sentence building

Use 'en mi casa, hay ...'
En mi casa, hay un cuarto de baño, una cocina ...
In my house there is a bathroom, a kitchen ...

Use a simple description

Mi casa es grande/pequeña.	My house is large/small.
Mi dormitorio es grande/pequeño.	My bedroom is large/small.
Mi dormitorio es azul.	My bedroom is blue.

Describe a fantasy house
En mi casa de imaginación hay cinco cuartos de baño y diez dormitorios.
In my fantasy house there are five bathrooms and ten bedrooms.

Ask a question
¿Cuál es tu habitación preferida?
What is your favourite room?

Sing a song
Reinforce vocabulary by singing a song such as 'En mi piso pequeño' from *¡Vamos a Cantar!*

Feliz Navidad

Key vocabulary

Feliz Navidad	Happy Christmas
Papá Noel	Father Christmas
Nochebuena	Christmas Eve
un árbol de Navidad	a Christmas tree
un muñeco de nieve	a snowman
un reno	a reindeer
un regalo	a present
los duendes	the elves
un adorno	a bauble
un pavo	turkey
la estrella	the star
un ángel	an angel
los Tres Reyes	the Three Kings
los pastores	the shepherds
el bebé Jesús	the baby Jesus
un establo	a stable
una cuna	a cradle

Feliz Navidad ✂ Matching cards

Feliz Navidad	**Happy Christmas**
Papá Noel	**Father Christmas**
un árbol de Navidad	a Christmas tree
un muñeco de nieve	a snowman
un regalo	a present
un reno	a reindeer

Feliz Navidad ✂ Matching cards

un ángel	an angel
los Tres Reyes	the Three Kings
los pastores	the shepherds
una cuna	a cradle
un adorno	a bauble
los duendes	the elves

Feliz Navidad

✂ Picture cards

Feliz Navidad	Happy Christmas
Papá Noel	
un árbol de Navidad	
un muñeco de nieve	
un regalo	
un reno	

Feliz Navidad

✂ Picture cards

un ángel	
los Tres Reyes	
los pastores	
una cuna	
un adorno	
los duendes	

Feliz Navidad Activity sheet

Nombre: .... Fecha: ....

I know some Christmas words in Spanish.
Draw lines to match up the English Christmas phrase to the correct Spanish phrase. Then draw a picture to match each Spanish phrase.

English	Spanish	Picture
Father Christmas	*un muñeco de nieve*	
a snowman	*los Tres Reyes*	
a Christmas tree	*un regalo*	
the Three Kings	*Papá Noel*	
a present	*un árbol de Navidad*	

Adicional

What colours does Papá Noel wear? Can you list them in Spanish?

Feliz Navidad

Puzzle page

Busca las palabras en la sopa de letras.
Search for the words in the grid.

Nochebuena
árbol
reno
regalo
duendes
pavo
estrella
ángel
pastores
establo
cuna

```
p e s t a b l o x c
a r á r b o l t r u
s x d u e n d e s n
t r e s t r e l l a
o i x p o x p i p x
r e g a l o s j r t
e e t r p a v o x b
s t n i x j r p i o
x r x o i á n g e l
n o c h e b u e n a
```

Descifra los anagramas.
Solve the anagrams.

áapp eonl   *Papá Noel*
un aeolgr   ....
nu nreo   ....
nu bálro   ....
al tseeallr   ....
nau nuca   ....

Conjeture.
Work it out.

_ _ / a _ _ _ _
_ n / r _ _ _
_ o _ / _ a _ t _ _ _ _   el árbol
u _ / e _ _ _ _ _ _
l _ _ / T _ _ _ / _ _ _ _ _

Une los dibujos con las palabras.
Match the words and pictures.

A   B   C

el arbol de Navidad   ....
Papá Noel   ....
el muñeco de nieve   ....

Feliz Navidad — Sentence building

Diseña una tarjeta de Navidad.
Make a Christmas or New Year card.

¡Feliz Navidad!	Happy Christmas
¡Feliz Año Nuevo!	Happy New Year
Querida Mamá	Dear Mum
Querido Papá	Dear Dad
Besos de	Love from

Use 'hay ...' to describe a nativity scene
Hay la estrella, el reno y los regalos. ...
There is the star, the reindeer and the shepherds ...

San Valentín

Key vocabulary

Feliz día de San Valentín	Happy Valentine's Day
Te Amo	I love you
Cásate conmigo	Marry me
Salga conmigo	Go out with me
mi novio	my boyfriend
mi novia	my girlfriend
un beso	a kiss
un corazón	a heart
un regalo	a present
una tarjeta	a card
las flores	flowers
bombones	chocolates
Cupido	Cupid

San Valentín ✂ Matching cards

San Valentín	Valentine's Day
Cupido	Cupid
bombones	chocolates
las flores	flowers
Te amo	I love you
Cásate conmigo	Marry me

San Valentín ✂ Matching cards

un beso	a kiss
un regalo	a present
una tarjeta	a card
mi novio	my boyfriend
mi novia	my girlfriend
Salga conmigo	Go out with me

San Valentín — Picture cards

Cupido	
bombones	
las flores	
Te amo	
un beso	
un regalo	
una tarjeta	
un corazón	

San Valentín Activity sheet

Nombre: .... Fecha: ....

I know some Valentine's Day words in Spanish.
Unscramble these words and write them correctly. Then draw a picture to match each word.

un aóorczn
....

aun aaerttj
....

un greaol
....

un seob
....

sal lfrose
....

bboomnse
....

doCpiu
....

Adicional

Now choose two words to scramble yourself. Write them here.

San Valentín

Puzzle page

Busca las palabras en la sopa de letras.
Search for the words in the grid.

novio	t	c	c	r	e	g	a	l	o	n
novia	a	b	o	m	b	o	n	e	s	o
beso	r	i	r	i	y	e	i	y	c	v
corazón	j	c	a	s	a	r	s	e	i	i
regalo	e	y	z	c	y	z	j	o	j	a
tarjeta	t	c	ó	c	u	p	i	d	o	z
flores	a	y	n	o	v	i	o	i	z	c
bombones	i	f	l	o	r	e	s	c	y	i
Cupido										

Descifra los anagramas.
Solve the anagrams.

odpuci   *Cupido*
sla serlof   ....
nu olgaer   ....
anu taejrat ....
un sebo   ....
et moa   ....

¿Qué es?
What is it?

u _ / t _ _ _ e _ _
m _ / _ _ _ _ a
_ _ _ b _ _ _ _
_ n / _ e _ _
u _ / c _ _ _ _ _ _

San Valentín — Sentence building

Hacer una tarjeta de San Valentín.
Make a Valentine's card.

Feliz día de San Valentín	Happy Valentine's Day
Querido Paul	Dear Paul
Querida Julie	Dear Julie
Te Amo	I love you
Besos de	Love from

Escribir una carta.
Write a letter.

Mi Cariño	Darling
Mi Amor	My love
Eres Bonita	You (female) are beautiful
Eres guapo	You are handsome
Te Amo	I love you
Besos	Kisses

Carnavales

Key vocabulary

una crepe	a pancake
un huevo	an egg
la leche	milk
la harina	flour
la mantequilla	butter
la sal	salt
una sartén	a pan
un traje	a costume
una fiesta	a party
una máscara	a mask
un desfile	a parade
una carroza	a float

Carnavales ✂ Matching cards

una crepe	a pancake
la mantequilla	butter
la harina	flour
un huevo	an egg
la leche	milk
una sartén	a pan

Carnavales

✂ Matching cards

la sal	salt
un traje	a costume
un desfile	a parade
una carroza	a float
una fiesta	a party
una máscara	a mask

Carnavales

✂ **Picture cards**

una crepe	
la mantequilla	
la harina	
un huevo	
la leche	
un sartén	

Carnavales — Picture cards

la sal	
un traje	
un desfile	
una carroza	
una fiesta	
una máscara	

Carnavales

Activity sheet

Nombre: .... Fecha: ....

I know some 'Carnavales' words in Spanish.
Draw and label the ingredients of a pancake in the bowl below. Use the vocabulary box to help you.

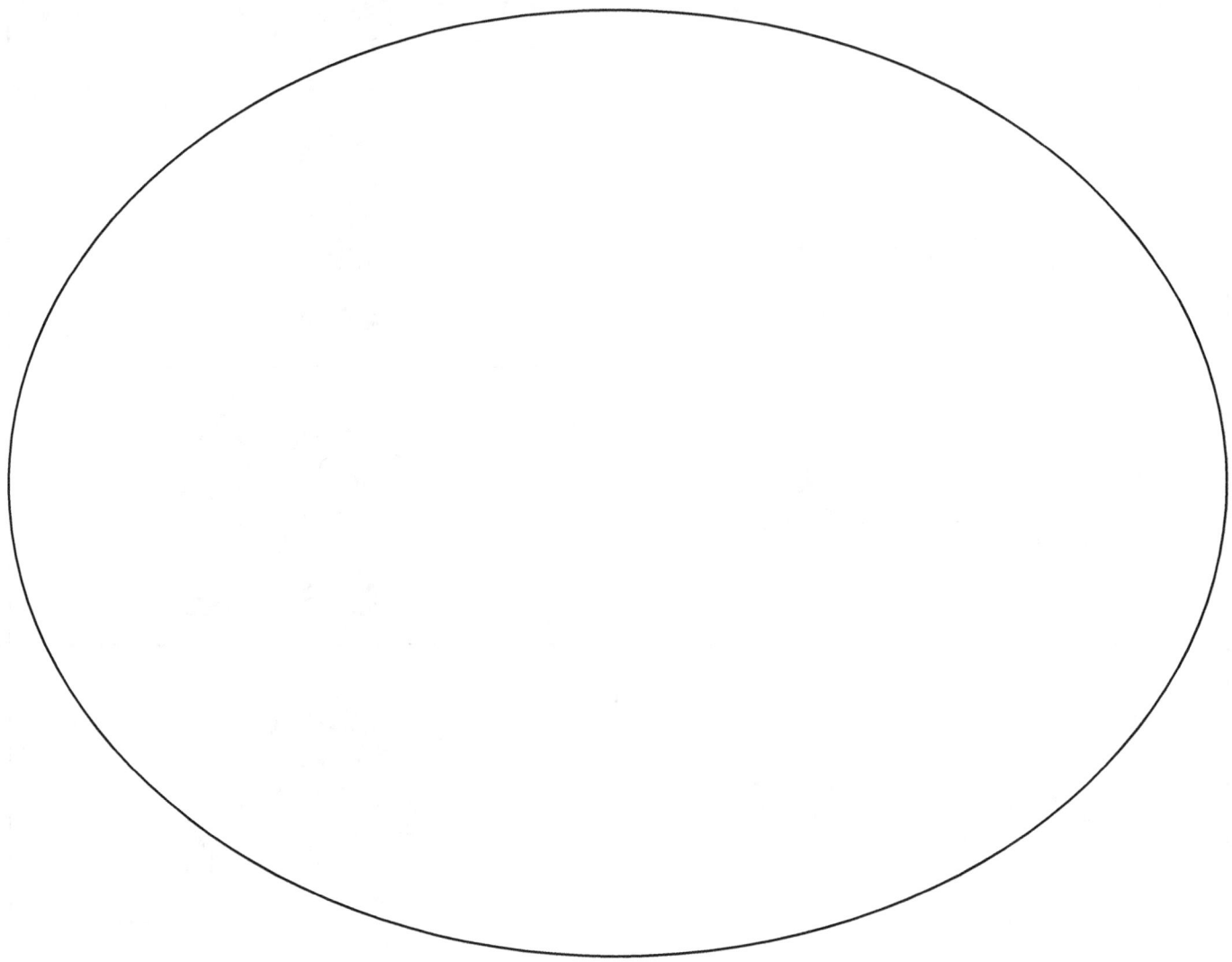

un huevo	an egg	**la leche**	milk
la harina	flour	**la mantequilla**	butter
la sal	salt		

Adicional

How many pancake toppings can you name, in Spanish?

Carnavales

Puzzle page

Busca las palabras en la sopa de letras.
Search for the words in the grid.

huevo
leche
harina
mantequilla
sal
sartén
traje
fiesta
máscara
desfile
carroza

```
d  i  s  t  r  a  j  e  j  s  o
j  c  a  r  r  o  z  a  q  a  h
m  a  n  t  e  q  u  i  l  l  a
á  j  o  v  o  q  h  q  e  o  r
s  a  r  t  é  n  o  v  c  h  i
c  h  o  q  h  q  v  q  h  v  n
a  v  d  e  s  f  i  l  e  q  a
r  o  q  f  i  e  s  t  a  h  j
a  j  h  u  e  v  o  j  h  v  q
```

Descifra los anagramas.
Solve the anagrams.

anu preec	una crepe
al lliauqtenma	....
al sla	....
al hriaan	....
nu uvohe	....
al hcele	....

Une los dibujos con las palabras.
Match the words and pictures.

A B C

una crepe ....
un huevo   ....
la leche   ....

Adivina?
Guess what?

u _ _ / _ _ _ p _   una crepe
_ a / l _ _ _ _
_ n _ / i _ _ _ _
_ _ _ / c _ _ _ _ _ _
_ n / _ _ _ f _ l _

Carnavales
Sentence building

Mime making a pancake using the recipe below.

Ponga el tamiz sobre el cuenco.	Put the sieve on top of the bowl.
Ponga la harina en el tamiz y en el cuenco.	Put the flour in the sieve and into the bowl.
Añada un poco de sal.	Add a little salt.
Ponga dos huevos en otro cuenco.	Put two eggs in another pot.
Ponga leche en el cuenco.	Put the milk in the pot.
Ponga los huevos y la leche en el cuenco con el azúcar.	Put the eggs and the milk in the bowl with the sugar.
Mezcle.	Mix.

Make a shopping list for pancakes.
Hay dos huevos, la leche ...
There are two eggs, some milk ...

Feliz Pascua

Key vocabulary

Feliz Pascua	Happy Easter
un conejo de Pascua	an Easter Bunny
un huevo de Pascua	an Easter egg
tableta de chocolate	bar of chocolate
una cesta	a basket
un narciso	a daffodil
un cordero	a lamb
un polluelo	a chick
una campana	a bell
una iglesia	a church
una caza del huevo de Pascua	an Easter egg hunt
primavera	spring

Feliz Pascua

✂ Matching cards

Feliz Pascua	**Happy Easter**
un conejo	**a rabbit**
tableta de chocolate	**bar of chocolate**
un huevo	**an egg**
una cesta	**a basket**
un narciso	**a daffodil**

Feliz Pascua

 Matching cards

un cordero	a lamb
un polluelo	a chick
una campana	a bell
una iglesia	a church
una caza del huevo de Pascua	an Easter egg hunt
primavera	spring

Feliz Pascua

✂ Picture cards

Feliz Pascua	
un conejo	
tableta de chocolate	
un huevo	
una cesta	
un narciso	

Feliz Pascua

✂ Picture cards

un cordero	
un polluelo	
una campana	
una iglesia	
una caza del huevo de Pascua	
primavera	

Feliz Pascua — Activity sheet

Nombre: .... Fecha: ....

I know some Easter words in Spanish.

Draw the Easter objects described below. Take care to colour them the right colour!

un conejo azul	una campana verde	un narciso naranja
un cordero blanco	un polluelo amarillo	una cesta roja
chocolate marrón	una iglesia negra	una campana ora

Adicional

Design **una gorra de Pascua** (an Easter bonnet) on the back of this sheet.

Feliz Pascua

Puzzle page

Busca las palabras en la sopa de letras.
Search for the words in the grid.

chocolate
cesta
narciso
cordero
polluelo
campana
iglesia
primavera

l	p	o	l	l	u	e	l	o	i
c	o	r	d	e	r	o	x	q	g
a	w	n	a	r	c	i	s	o	l
m	c	h	o	c	o	l	a	t	e
p	l	e	a	f	e	s	t	v	s
a	m	b	s	t	r	e	n	t	i
n	o	l	p	t	h	b	u	n	a
a	p	r	i	m	a	v	e	r	a

Descifra los anagramas.
Solve the anagrams.

nu ojenco	*un conejo*
talocohce	....
nau staec	....
nu osicran	....
aun glieias	....
un lloopue	....

¿Quién soy?
Who am I?

A yellow flower.	*un narciso*
I hop.	....
I'm yellow and fluffy.	....
I ring.	....
I'm delicious.	....

Feliz Pascua — Sentence building

Describe Easter using 'hay ...'

Hay un conejo de Pascua, un huevo, dos corderos ...
There is an Easter Bunny, an egg, two lambs ...

Make an Easter card

¡Feliz Pascua!	Happy Easter
Querida Mamá	Dear Mum
Querido Papá	Dear Dad
Besos de	Love from

FELIZ PASCUA

Todos los Santos

Key vocabulary

un fantasma	a ghost
una calavera	a skull
un traje	a costume
un vampiro	a vampire
un gato negro	a black cat
un esqueleto	a skeleton
una casa embrujada	a haunted house
una bruja	a witch
una araña	a spider
una calabaza	a pumpkin
caramelos	sweets
un murciélago	a bat

Todos los Santos ✂ Matching cards

un fantasma	a ghost
una calavera	a skull
un traje	a costume
un vampiro	a vampire
una casa embrujada	a haunted house
una bruja	a witch

Todos los Santos  Matching cards

un gato negro	a black cat
un esqueleto	a skeleton
caramelos	sweets
una araña	a spider
una calabaza	a pumpkin
un murciélago	a bat

Todos los Santos ✂ Picture cards

un fantasma	
una calavera	
un traje	
un vampiro	
una casa embrujada	
una bruja	

Todos los Santos ✂ Picture cards

un gato negro	
un esqueleto	
caramelos	
una araña	
una calabaza	
un murciélago	

Todos los Santos — Activity sheet

Nombre: .... *Fecha:* ....

I know some Halloween words in Spanish.

Draw the outline of a large haunted house below. Then draw and label some spooky Halloween objects inside it. Use the vocabulary box to help you.

un fantasma	a ghost	***una calavera***	a skull
un traje	a costume	***un vampiro***	a vampire
un gato negro	a black cat	***un esqueleto***	a skeleton
un murciélago	a bat	***una bruja***	a witch
una calabaza	a pumpkin	***una araña***	a spider
caramelos	sweets	***una casa embrujada***	a haunted house

Todos los Santos — Puzzle page

Busca las palabras en la sopa de letras.
Search for the words in the grid.

fantasma
calavera
traje
vampiro
esqueleto
bruja
araña
caramelos
calabaza
murciélago

```
z x t v a m p i r o
m u r c i é l a g o
b q a z w q z x f q
r z j q a r a ñ a z
u q e z x q w r n w
j e s q u e l e t o
a c a l a b a z a w
c a r a m e l o s x
z w x q z r x r m q
x c a l a v e r a x
```

Descifra los anagramas.
Solve the anagrams.

aun aaclaazb — una calabaza
nu teelouesq — ....
macraelos — ....
nu tgoa groen — ....
nu oripmav — ....
anu jabru — ....

¿Qué es?
What is it?

_ _ / f _ _ _ a _ _ _   un fantasma
_ _ a / _ r _ _ _
_ _ / _ _ _ o / _ e _ _ o
u _ _ / b _ _ _ _
_ n _ / c _ _ _ _ _ _ _

Une los dibujos con las palabras.
Match the words and pictures.

A   B   C

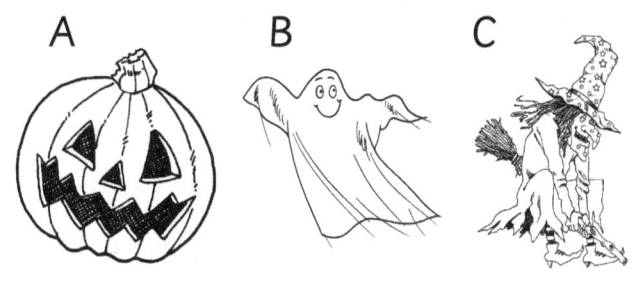

un fantasma ....
una bruja ....
una calabaza ....

¿Quién es?
Who is it?

I ride on my broomstick — una bruja
I am a black animal — ....
I am orange — ....
I have some big teeth — ....
I live in a web — ....

Todos los Santos — Sentence building

Describe the haunted house you have drawn on the activity sheet
En mi casa embrujada, hay ...
In my haunted house there is ...

Charades
Children could pull a Halloween word out of a hat and mime the word. Children are to guess it in Spanish:

¿Es un vampiro?   Is it a vampire?

Sí/no.   Yes/no

Write a song
Children could write a spooky song listing Halloween words, to the tune of 'Head, shoulders, knees and toes'; they could add their own actions and perform it to the class.

Ages: 5–11yrs

Lotto en Español

A Fun Way to Reinforce Spanish Vocabulary

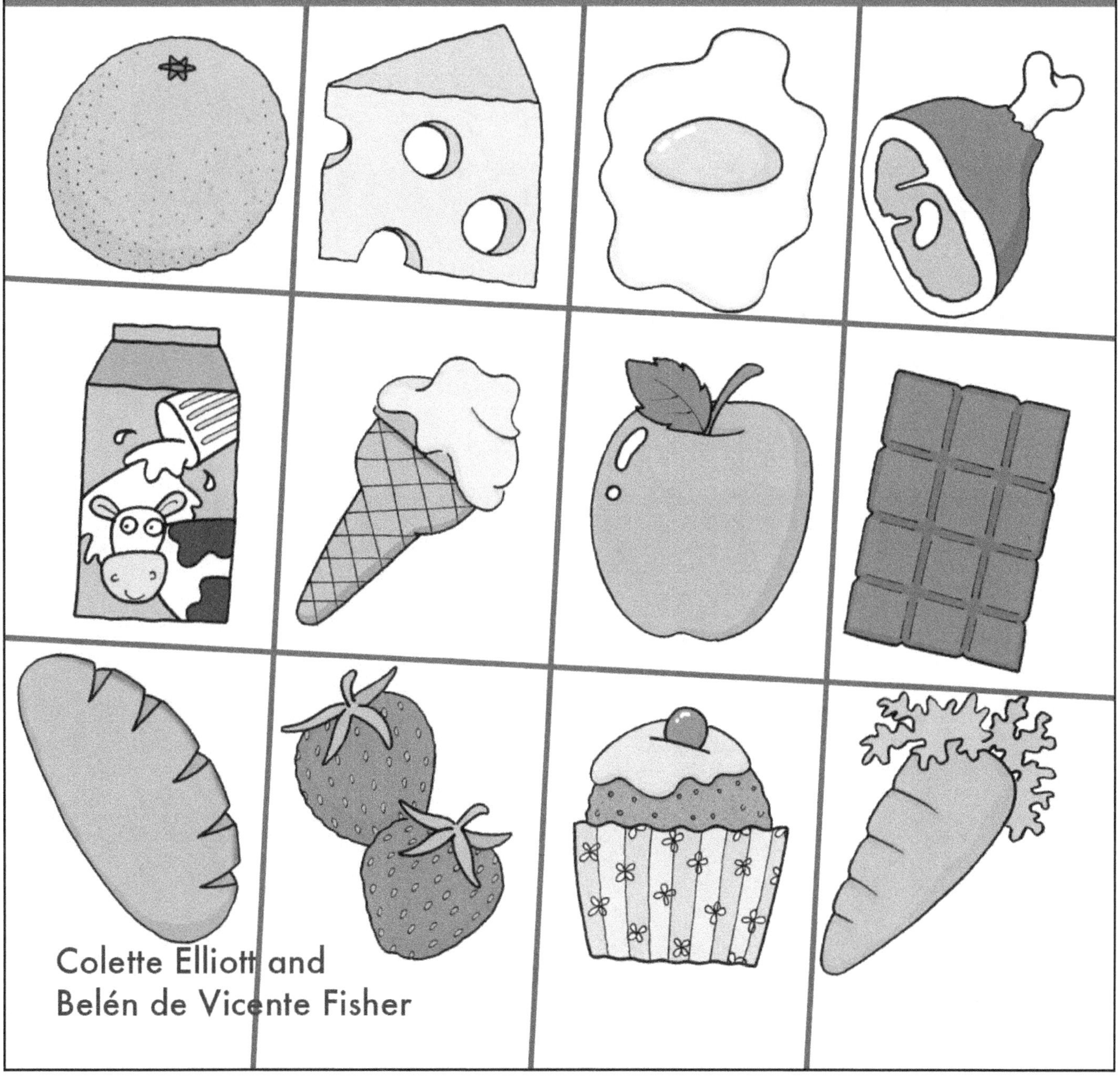

Colette Elliott and
Belén de Vicente Fisher

Lotto en Español

A Fun Way to Reinforce Spanish Vocabulary

Colette Elliott and Belén de Vicente Fisher

We hope you and your pupils enjoy playing the lotto games in this book. Brilliant Publications publishes many other books for teaching modern foreign languages. To find out more details on any of the titles listed below, please go to our website: www.brilliantpublications.co.uk.

100+ Fun Ideas for Practising Modern Foreign Languages in the Primary Classroom	978-1-903853-98-6
More Fun Ideas for Advancing Modern Foreign Languages in the Primary Classroom	978-1-905780-72-3
¡Es Español!	978-1-903853-64-1
Juguemos Todos Juntos	978-1-903853-95-5
¡Vamos a Cantar!	978-1-905780-13-6
Spanish Pen Pals Made Easy	978-1-905780-42-6
Spanish Festivals and Traditions	978-1-905780-53-2
Buena Idea	978-1-905780-63-1
Chantez Plus Fort!	978-1-903853-37-5
Hexagonie 1	978-1-905780-59-4
Hexagonie 2	978-1-905780-18-1
Jouons Tous Ensemble	978-1-903853-81-8
C'est Français!	978-1-903853-02-3
J'aime Chanter!	978-1-905780-11-2
J'aime Parler!	978-1-905780-12-9
French Pen Pals Made Easy	978-1-905780-10-5
Loto Français	978-1-905780-45-7
French Festivals and Traditions	978-1-905780-44-0
Bonne Idée	978-1-905780-62-4
Unforgettable French	978-1-78317-093-7
Das ist Deutsch	978-1-905780-15-0
Wir Spielen Zusammen	978-1-903853-97-9
German Pen Pals Made Easy	978-1-905780-43-3
German Festivals and Traditions	978-1-905780-85-3
Deutsch-Lotto	978-1-905780-46-4
Gute Idee	978-1-905780-65-5
Giochiamo Tutti Insieme	978-1-903853-96-2
Lotto in Italiano	978-1-905780-48-8
Buon'Idea	978-0-85747-696-8

Published by Brilliant Publications Limited
Unit 10
Sparrow Hall Farm
Edlesborough
Dunstable
Bedfordshire
LU6 2ES, UK

General information enquiries:
Tel: 01525 222292

The name Brilliant Publications and the logo are registered trademarks.

Written by Colette Elliott and Belén de Vicente Fisher
Illustrated by Gaynor Berry
Front cover designed by Brilliant Publications

© Text Colette Elliott and Belén de Vicente Fisher 2009
© Design Brilliant Publications 2009

Printed ISBN: 978-1-905780-47-1
ebook ISBN: 978-1-905780-99-0

First printed and published in the UK in 2009

The right of Colette Elliott and Belén de Vicente Fisher to be identified as the authors of this work has been asserted by themselves in accordance with the Copyright, Designs and Patents Act 1988.

Pages 7–57 may be photocopied by individual teachers acting on behalf of the purchasing institution for classroom use only, without permission from the publisher and without declaration to the Copyright Licensing Agency or Publishers' Licensing Services. The materials may not be reproduced in any other form or for any other purpose without the prior permission of the publisher.

Contents

Introduction 4
How to play 5
Different ways of playing/ideas 6

Los números del 1 al 12 (Numbers 1–12)
    Call sheet 8
    Picture only boards 9–10
    Pictures and words boards 11–12
    Words only boards 13–14

Los números del 1 al 60 (Numbers 1–60)
    Call sheet 15
    Picture only boards 16–17
    Pictures and words boards 18–19
    Words only boards 20–21

Los animales (Animals)
    Call sheet 22
    Picture only boards 23–24
    Pictures and words boards 25–26
    Words only boards 27–28

¡Que aproveche! (Food)
    Call sheet 29
    Picture only boards 30–31
    Pictures and words boards 32–33
    Words only boards 34–35

En la clase (Classroom objects)
    Call sheet 36
    Picture only boards 37–38
    Pictures and words boards 39–40
    Words only boards 41–42

La ropa (Clothes)
    Call sheet 43
    Picture only boards 44–45
    Pictures and words boards 46–47
    Words only boards 48–49

La Navidad (Christmas)
    Call sheet 50
    Picture only boards 51–52
    Pictures and words boards 53–54
    Words only boards 55–56

Blank template boards 57
List of vocabulary used in games 58

Introduction

The perennially popular game of lotto is an enjoyable and effective way to teach and/or reinforce vocabulary and language structures. It can be used as a teaching tool or as a fun follow-up activity after a lesson. It provides a stimulating and meaningful way to develop reading, listening and speaking skills.

The games in *Lotto en Español* can be played in a variety of ways (see pages 5–7) and with very little preparation from you. There is no need to give the children counters or individual cards. Simply photocopy the boards, hand them out to your pupils together with some colouring pencils and, bingo, you can start playing!

Our unique call sheets provide the 'order of call' and enable you to follow the game closely and to select which team you want to win.

Lotto can be played in small groups, or with an entire class. There is no limit to the number of players and the games are suitable for ages four upwards.

There are seven topics in *Lotto en Español*:
- Los números del 1 al 12   Numbers 1–12
- Los números del 1 al 60   Numbers 1–60
- Los animales   Animals
- ¡Que aproveche!   Food
- En la clase   Classroom objects
- La ropa   Clothes
- La Navidad   Christmas

For each topic there are three versions of the boards, allowing maximum flexibility, particularly in mixed ability classes.

pictures only   words and pictures   words only

The ideas in this book are by no means exhaustive and, should you decide to cut the boards to make flashcards or playing cards, then the number of games is unlimited!

Have fun playing!

How to play

Getting started
For each topic, in each format, there are four different numbered boards, so you can play with four teams. Just photocopy the sheets, cut them in half, and hand out the boards to the children. For a class of 28 pupils, you only need to copy two pages seven times each.

It is a good idea to go through the vocabulary with the children before playing. The best way to do this is either to scan and place the four boards on the whiteboard, or enlarge the 12 pictures on the photocopier and use them as flashcards.

Make sure that the boards are evenly distributed throughout the class. After giving the boards out and before you start playing, ask for a show of hands to see how the teams are spread out in the classroom. The children like to see who is in their team and this increases the element of competition!

How to play
Each topic contains a call sheet, with the words numbered 1 to 12. The caller can start calling from any number. The white area in the table indicates who the winning board will be.

The children can play on their own or in pairs for moral support.

The winner is the first child to shout 'lotto' (hopefully the rest of that team will also shout 'lotto', but the real winner is the child who shouts out first). Get the winner to say all the words in Spanish whilst you check on the list. This is a good reading/speaking exercise.

Once the first team has won, you can stop the game or carry on until everyone has shouted 'lotto' (you will know from the call sheet who the next winner will be).

You can play several games with the same boards by marking the boards in different ways:
◆ Colour the box outline (or only one side of the box if you want to make it last!)
◆ Colour the picture
◆ Colour the background
◆ Tick or cross the box, etc.

It is best to tell the children to shout 'lotto' as soon as the caller says the word, rather than wait until the colouring is done, as this may cause arguments amongst the children!

Variations
Instead of evenly distributing the boards, you could make it a competition within the class: divide the class into four groups, give the same boards to each group, and see which group says 'lotto' first.

Children could play in groups of five. One child is the caller (give him/her a photocopy of the call list) and the others use four different boards. Only one winner this time!

The order of call is the same for all the topics, so you can play 'mix and match' games with different topics. If you decide to do so, make sure that the four different teams are evenly spread.

Different ways of playing/ideas

- Call the words from the call sheet in Spanish. Start anywhere, but make a note of where you started on a separate sheet of paper. Alternatively, get a child to do the calling. Assist him/her with the more difficult words.

- The children take it in turns to call out an item from their own board in Spanish. When they call a word, they colour their own picture and everybody who has that picture says 'gracias' and colours their picture. Then the child sitting next to the caller says the next word, etc. This is a very good reading exercise if the 'words only' boards are used. The teacher should make a note of which items have been called on the call sheet.

- Call the words in English, and the children have to find the Spanish translation (this can only be played with the 'words only' boards).

- Show a picture without saying anything (using the 'words only' boards).

- Write a word on the board without saying anything (for 'pictures only' boards).

- Instead of using the call sheets, photocopy the boards and cut them up into cards, then pick the cards out of a hat. The pupils could take turns to pick a card and call out the word.

- Ask the children to colour the pictures before playing and then call the words with a colour, eg "un gato rojo". To keep the game from lasting too long, limit the children to the same two colours. (You can use the two columns on the call sheets to indicate the colour. For example, write A for "azul" at the top of the list of Spanish words and R for "rojo" at the top of the English word list.)

- Give a description of the word in Spanish.

- For the number "lotto" boards, give sums for the children to work out.

- Spell the words.

- Give a rhyming word.

- Include the word in a sentence eg un caramelo; un caramelo por favor; por favor me puedes dar un caramelo; buenos dias señora, me puede dar un caramelo por favor.

- Make the game last the whole lesson. Give the boards at the beginning and call the words at intervals during the lesson, either on their own or in a sentence.

- Give everybody the same board. Each child has to preselect four items by circling or colouring them.

- Give the children the blank template board (pages 57) and get them to write/draw their own items/numbers from a list you have given on the board. This can be played with any topic/structures/verbs/grammar.

- Make the children repeat the word several times whilst they are colouring.

- The children ask each other a question each time, eg:

    - ¿Qué te gustaría? What would you like?

    - ¿Cuántos? ¿Qué número es? How many? What number?
      ¿Qué número quieres? You'd like what number?

    - ¿Qué es esto? What is this?

    - ¿Qué estás comiendo? What are you eating?

    - ¿Tienes animales/mascotas? Do you have an animal/pets?

    - ¿Qué llevas puesto? What are you wearing?

- If you photocopy the boards double-sided, they will last even longer.

Los números del 1 al 12

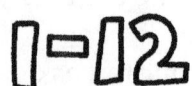

Team 1 to win	Start on 2 or 7
Team 2 to win	Start on 1, 3, 4 or 12
Team 3 to win	Start on 3, 5, 7, 10 or 11
Team 4 to win	Start on 5, 7, 8 or 9
All teams to win	Start on 6

These numbers refer to the numbers on the left and right of the grid below.

Tick the white boxes in the grid as you call out the words.

				Winning team										
				2	1	2&3	2	3&4	All	1,3,4	4	4	3	3	2	
Order of call	1	cinco	five													1
	2	nueve	nine													2
	3	once	eleven													3
	4	dos	two													4
	5	cuatro	four													5
	6	doce	twelve													6
	7	tres	three													7
	8	uno	one													8
	9	seis	six													9
	10	ocho	eight													10
	11	diez	ten													11
	12	siete	seven													12
	1	cinco	five													1
	2	nueve	nine													2
	3	once	eleven													3
	4	dos	two													4
	5	cuatro	four													5
	6	doce	twelve													6
	7	tres	three													7
	8	uno	one													8
	9	seis	six													9

Lotto en Español

© Colette Elliott, Belén de Vicente Fisher and Brilliant Publications Limited.
This board may be photocopied for use by the purchaser.

¡Lotto! (Tablero 1) Nombre: _____   1-12

2	8	9
3	1	4

Lotto en Español – Los números del 1 al 12

© Colette Elliott, Belén de Vicente Fisher and Brilliant Publications Limited.
This board may be photocopied for use by the purchaser.

¡Lotto! (Tablero 2) Nombre: _____   1-12

1	5	6
4	12	2

Lotto en Español – Los números del 1 al 12

© Colette Elliott, Belén de Vicente Fisher and Brilliant Publications Limited.
This board may be photocopied for use by the purchaser.

¡Lotto! (Tablero 3) Nombre: _____ 1-12

7	5	10
11	3	4

Lotto en Español – Los números del 1 al 12

© Colette Elliott, Belén de Vicente Fisher and Brilliant Publications Limited.
This board may be photocopied for use by the purchaser.

¡Lotto! (Tablero 4) Nombre: _____ 1-12

11	4	6
7	8	9

Lotto en Español – Los números del 1 al 12

© Colette Elliott, Belén de Vicente Fisher and Brilliant Publications Limited.
This board may be photocopied for use by the purchaser.

¡Lotto! (Tablero 1)   Nombre: _____   1-12

2 dos	8 ocho	9 nueve
3 tres	1 uno	4 cuatro

Lotto en Español – Los números del 1 al 12

© Colette Elliott, Belén de Vicente Fisher and Brilliant Publications Limited.
This board may be photocopied for use by the purchaser.

¡Lotto! (Tablero 2)   Nombre: _____   1-12

1 uno	5 cinco	6 seis
4 cuatro	12 doce	2 dos

Lotto en Español – Los números del 1 al 12

© Colette Elliott, Belén de Vicente Fisher and Brilliant Publications Limited.
This board may be photocopied for use by the purchaser.

¡Lotto! (Tablero 3) Nombre: _____ 1-12

7 siete	5 cinco	10 diez
11 once	3 tres	4 cuatro

Lotto en Español – Los números del 1 al 12

© Colette Elliott, Belén de Vicente Fisher and Brilliant Publications Limited.
This board may be photocopied for use by the purchaser.

¡Lotto! (Tablero 4) Nombre: _____ 1-12

11 once	4 cuatro	6 seis
7 siete	8 ocho	9 nueve

Lotto en Español – Los números del 1 al 12

© Colette Elliott, Belén de Vicente Fisher and Brilliant Publications Limited.
This board may be photocopied for use by the purchaser.

¡Lotto! (Tablero 1)   Nombre: _____   1-12

doce	ocho	nueve
tres	uno	cuatro

Lotto en Español – Los números del 1 al 12

¡Lotto! (Tablero 2)   Nombre: _____   1-12

uno	cinco	seis
cuatro	doce	dos

Lotto en Español – Los números del 1 al 12

¡Lotto! (Tablero 3) Nombre: _____ 1-12

siete	cinco	diez
once	tres	cuatro

Lotto en Español – Los números del 1 al 12

© Colette Elliott, Belén de Vicente Fisher and Brilliant Publications Limited.
This board may be photocopied for use by the purchaser.

¡Lotto! (Tablero 4) Nombre: _____ 1-12

once	cuatro	seis
siete	ocho	nueve

Lotto en Español – Los números del 1 al 12

© Colette Elliott, Belén de Vicente Fisher and Brilliant Publications Limited.
This board may be photocopied for use by the purchaser.

Los números del 1 al 60

Team 1 to win	Start on 2 or 7
Team 2 to win	Start on 1, 3, 4 or 12
Team 3 to win	Start on 3, 5, 7, 10 or 11
Team 4 to win	Start on 5, 7, 8 or 9
All teams to win	Start on 6

These numbers refer to the numbers on the left and right of the grid below.

Tick the white boxes in the grid as you call out the words.

				Winning team											
				2	1	2&3	2	3&4	All	1,3,4	4	4	3	3	2	
Order of call	1	veintiséis	twenty-six													1
	2	siete	seven													2
	3	sesenta	sixty													3
	4	treinta y cinco	thirty-five													4
	5	cincuenta y ocho	fifty-eight													5
	6	cuarenta y uno	forty-one													6
	7	quince	fifteen													7
	8	cincuenta	fifty													8
	9	doce	twelve													9
	10	cuarenta y dos	forty-two													10
	11	treinta y cuatro	thirty-four													11
	12	diecinueve	nineteen													12
	1	veintiséis	twenty-six													1
	2	siete	seven													2
	3	sesenta	sixty													3
	4	treinta y cinco	thirty-five													4
	5	cincuenta y ocho	fifty-eight													5
	6	cuarenta y uno	forty-one													6
	7	quince	fifteen													7
	8	cincuenta	fifty													8
	9	doce	twelve													9

¡Lotto! (Tablero 1)   Nombre: _____   1-60

35	42	7
15	50	58

Lotto en Español – Los números del 1 al 60

© Colette Elliott, Belén de Vicente Fisher and Brilliant Publications Limited.
This board may be photocopied for use by the purchaser.

¡Lotto! (Tablero 2)   Nombre: _____   1-60

50	26	12
58	41	35

Lotto en Español – Los números del 1 al 60

© Colette Elliott, Belén de Vicente Fisher and Brilliant Publications Limited.
This board may be photocopied for use by the purchaser.

¡Lotto! (Tablero 3) Nombre: _____ 1-60

19	26	34
60	15	58

Lotto en Español – Los números del 1 al 60

© Colette Elliott, Belén de Vicente Fisher and Brilliant Publications Limited.
This board may be photocopied for use by the purchaser.

¡Lotto! (Tablero 4) Nombre: _____ 1-60

60	58	12
19	42	7

Lotto en Español – Los números del 1 al 60

© Colette Elliott, Belén de Vicente Fisher and Brilliant Publications Limited.
This board may be photocopied for use by the purchaser.

¡Lotto! (Tablero 1) Nombre: _____ 1-60

35 treinta y cinco	42 cuarenta y dos	7 siete
15 quince	50 cincuenta	58 cincuenta y ocho

¡Lotto! (Tablero 2) Nombre: _____ 1-60

50 cincuenta	26 veintiséis	12 doce
58 cincuenta y ocho	41 cuarenta y uno	35 treinta y cinco

¡Lotto! (Tablero 3) Nombre: _____   1-60

| 19 diecinueve | 26 veintiséis | 34 treinta y cuatro |
| 60 sesenta | 15 quince | 58 cincuenta y ocho |

Lotto en Español – Los números del 1 al 60

¡Lotto! (Tablero 4) Nombre: _____   1-60

| 60 sesenta | 58 cincuenta y ocho | 12 doce |
| 19 diecinueve | 42 cuarenta y dos | 7 siete |

¡Lotto! (Tablero 1)   Nombre: _____   1-60

treinta y cinco	cuarenta y dos	siete
quince	cincuenta	cincuenta y ocho

Lotto en Español – Los números del 1 al 60

© Colette Elliott, Belén de Vicente Fisher and Brilliant Publications Limited.
This board may be photocopied for use by the purchaser.

¡Lotto! (Tablero 2)   Nombre: _____   1-60

cincuenta	veintiséis	doce
cincuenta y ocho	cuarenta y uno	treinta y cinco

¡Lotto! (Tablero 3)   Nombre: _____   1-60

diecinueve	veintiséis	treinta y cinco
sesenta	quince	cincuenta y ocho

Lotto en Español – Los números del 1 al 60

¡Lotto! (Tablero 4)   Nombre: _____   1-60

sesenta	cincuenta y ocho	doce
diecinueve	cuarenta y dos	siete

Lotto en Español – Los números del 1 al 60

Los animales

Team 1 to win	Start on 2 or 7
Team 2 to win	Start on 1, 3, 4 or 12
Team 3 to win	Start on 3, 5, 7, 10 or 11
Team 4 to win	Start on 5, 7, 8 or 9
All teams to win	Start on 6

These numbers refer to the numbers on the left and right of the grid below.

Tick the white boxes in the grid as you call out the words.

				Winning team											
				2	1	2&3	2	3&4	All	1,3,4	4	4	3	3	2	
Order of call	1	un cerdo	a pig													1
	2	un ratón	a mouse													2
	3	una cobaya	a guinea pig													3
	4	una vaca	a cow													4
	5	un hámster	a hamster													5
	6	un caballo	a horse													6
	7	un conejo	a rabbit													7
	8	un gato	a cat													8
	9	un perro	a dog													9
	10	un pez	a goldfish													10
	11	un pato	a duck													11
	12	una gallina	a hen													12
	1	un cerdo	a pig													1
	2	un ratón	a mouse													2
	3	una cobaya	a guinea pig													3
	4	una vaca	a cow													4
	5	un hámster	a hamster													5
	6	un caballo	a horse													6
	7	un conejo	a rabbit													7
	8	un gato	a cat													8
	9	un perro	a dog													9

¡Lotto! (Tablero 1)   Nombre: _____

Lotto en Español – Los animales

© *Colette Elliott, Belén de Vicente Fisher and Brilliant Publications Limited.*
This board may be photocopied for use by the purchaser.

¡Lotto! (Tablero 2)   Nombre: _____

Lotto en Español – Los animales

© *Colette Elliott, Belén de Vicente Fisher and Brilliant Publications Limited.*
This board may be photocopied for use by the purchaser.

¡Lotto! (Tablero 3) Nombre: _____

Lotto en Español – Los animales

© Colette Elliott, Belén de Vicente Fisher and Brilliant Publications Limited.
This board may be photocopied for use by the purchaser.

¡Lotto! (Tablero 4) Nombre: _____

Lotto en Español – Los animales

© Colette Elliott, Belén de Vicente Fisher and Brilliant Publications Limited.
This board may be photocopied for use by the purchaser.

¡Lotto! (Tablero 1)   Nombre: _____

 una vaca	 un pez	 un ratón
 un conejo	 un gato	 un hámster

Lotto en Español – Los animales

¡Lotto! (Tablero 2)   Nombre: _____

 un gato	 un cerdo	 un perro
 un hámster	 un caballo	 una vaca

Lotto en Español – Los animales

¡Lotto! (Tablero 3) Nombre: _____

una gallina

un cerdo

un pato

una cobaya

un conejo

un hámster

¡Lotto! (Tablero 4) Nombre: _____

una cobaya

un hámster

un perro

una gallina

un pez

un ratón

¡Lotto! (Tablero 1) Nombre: _____

una vaca	un pez	un ratón
un conejo	un gato	un hámster

Lotto en Español – Los animales

¡Lotto! (Tablero 2) Nombre: _____

un gato	un cerdo	un perro
un hámster	un caballo	una vaca

Lotto en Español – Los animales

¡Lotto! (Tablero 3) Nombre: _____

una gallina	un cerdo	un pato
una cobaya	un conejo	un hámster

¡Lotto! (Tablero 4) Nombre: _____

una cobaya	un hámster	un perro
una gallina	un pez	un ratón

¡Que aproveche!

Team 1 to win	Start on 2 or 7
Team 2 to win	Start on 1, 3, 4 or 12
Team 3 to win	Start on 3, 5, 7, 10 or 11
Team 4 to win	Start on 5, 7, 8 or 9
All teams to win	Start on 6

These numbers refer to the numbers on the left and right of the grid below.

Tick the white boxes in the grid as you call out the words.

				Winning team											
				2	1	2&3	2	3&4	All	1,3,4	4	4	3	3	2	
Order of call	1	una tarta	a cake													1
	2	una manzana	an apple													2
	3	un helado	an ice-cream													3
	4	un poco de queso	some cheese													4
	5	un pollo	a chicken													5
	6	una patata	a potato													6
	7	un brik de leche	a carton of milk													7
	8	un jamón	a ham													8
	9	un huevo	an egg													9
	10	unas patatas fritas	some chips													10
	11	un poco de pan	some bread													11
	12	unos caramelos	some sweets													12
	1	una tarta	a cake													1
	2	una manzana	an apple													2
	3	un helado	an ice-cream													3
	4	un poco de queso	some cheese													4
	5	un pollo	a chicken													5
	6	una patata	a potato													6
	7	un brik de leche	a carton of milk													7
	8	un jamón	a ham													8
	9	un huevo	an egg													9

Lotto en Español

¡Lotto! (Tablero 1)   Nombre: _____

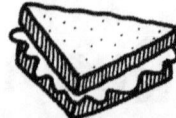

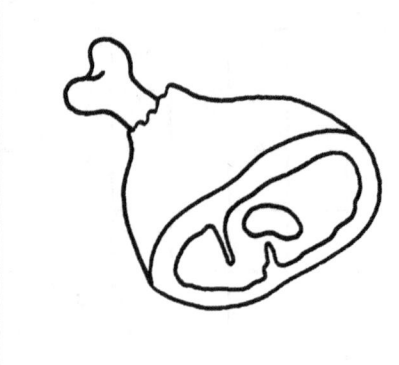

Lotto en Español – ¡Que aproveche! © Colette Elliott, Belén de Vicente Fisher and Brilliant Publications Limited.
This board may be photocopied for use by the purchaser.

¡Lotto! (Tablero 2)   Nombre: _____

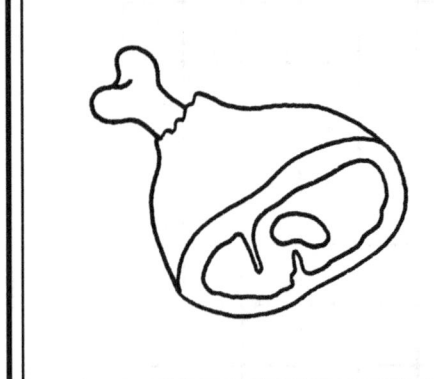

Lotto en Español – ¡Que aproveche! © Colette Elliott, Belén de Vicente Fisher and Brilliant Publications Limited.
This board may be photocopied for use by the purchaser.

¡Lotto! (Tablero 3) Nombre: _____

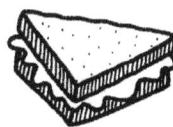

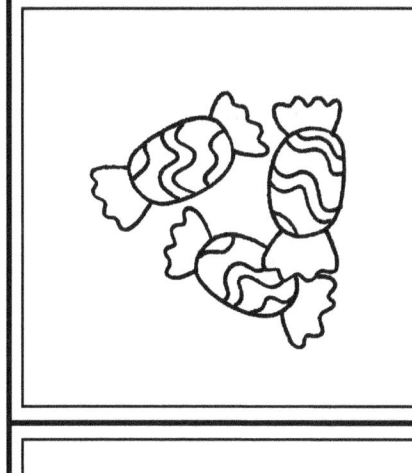  

Lotto en Español – ¡Que aproveche! © Colette Elliott, Belén de Vicente Fisher and Brilliant Publications Limited.
This board may be photocopied for use by the purchaser.

¡Lotto! (Tablero 4) Nombre: _____

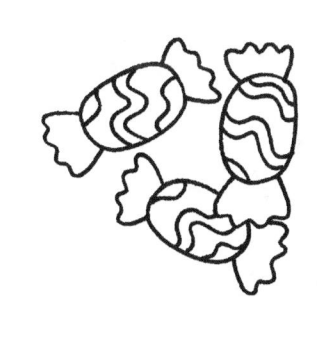  

Lotto en Español – ¡Que aproveche! © Colette Elliott, Belén de Vicente Fisher and Brilliant Publications Limited.
This board may be photocopied for use by the purchaser.

¡Lotto! (Tablero 1)   Nombre: _____

un poco de queso	unas patatas fritas	una manzana
	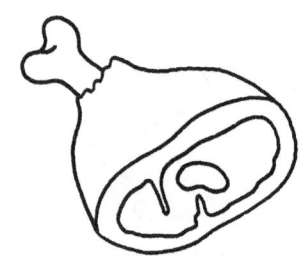	
un brik de leche	un jamón	un pollo

¡Lotto! (Tablero 2)   Nombre: _____

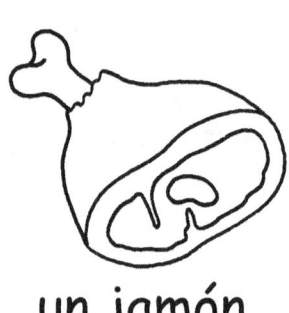		
un jamón	una tarta	un huevo
	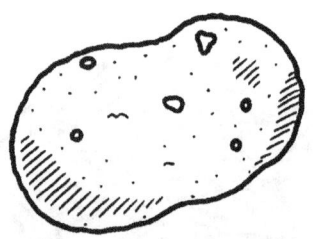	
un pollo	una patata	un poco de queso

¡Lotto! (Tablero 3) Nombre: _____

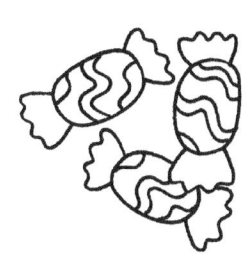 unos caramelos	 una tarta	 un poco de pan
 un helado	 un brik de leche	 un pollo

Lotto en Español – ¡Que aproveche!

¡Lotto! (Tablero 4) Nombre: _____

 un helado	 un pollo	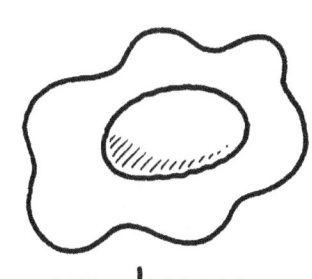 un huevo
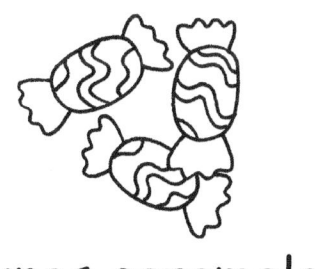 unos caramelos	 unas patatas fritas	 una manzana

Lotto en Español – ¡Que aproveche!

¡Lotto! (Tablero 1)   Nombre: _____

un poco de queso	unas patatas fritas	una manzana
un brik de leche	un jamón	un pollo

¡Lotto! (Tablero 2)   Nombre: _____

un jamón	una tarta	un huevo
un pollo	una patata	un poco de queso

¡Lotto! (Tablero 3) Nombre: _____

unos caramelos	una tarta	un poco de pan
un helado	un brik de leche	un pollo

Lotto en Español – ¡Que aproveche!

¡Lotto! (Tablero 4) Nombre: _____

un helado	un pollo	un huevo
unos caramelos	unas patatas fritas	una manzana

Lotto en Español – ¡Que aproveche!

En la clase

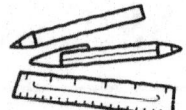

Team 1 to win	Start on 2 or 7
Team 2 to win	Start on 1, 3, 4 or 12
Team 3 to win	Start on 3, 5, 7, 10 or 11
Team 4 to win	Start on 5, 7, 8 or 9
All teams to win	Start on 6

These numbers refer to the numbers on the left and right of the grid below.

Tick the white boxes in the grid as you call out the words.

				Winning team											
				2	1	2&3	2	3&4	All	1,3,4	4	4	3	3	2	
Order of call	1	un libro	a book													1
	2	un sacapuntas	a pencil sharpener													2
	3	una regla	a ruler													3
	4	una mochila	a school bag													4
	5	unas tijeras	some scissors													5
	6	un lápiz	a pencil													6
	7	una goma	a rubber													7
	8	un cuaderno	a workbook													8
	9	un bolígrafo	a pen													9
	10	un estuche	a pencil case													10
	11	una calculadora	a calculator													11
	12	una barra de pegamento	a glue stick													12
	1	un libro	a book													1
	2	un sacapuntas	a pencil sharpener													2
	3	una regla	a ruler													3
	4	una mochila	a school bag													4
	5	unas tijeras	some scissors													5
	6	un lápiz	a pencil													6
	7	una goma	a rubber													7
	8	un cuaderno	a workbook													8
	9	un bolígrafo	a pen													9

¡Lotto! (Tablero 1)   Nombre: _____

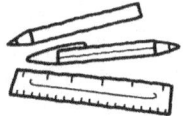

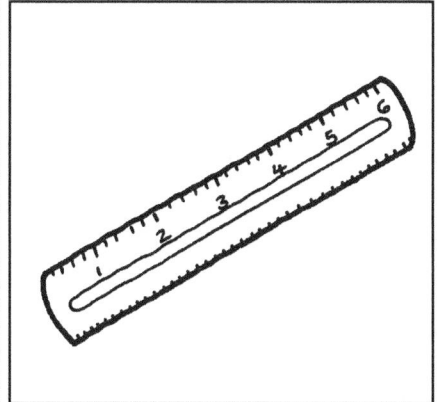  

Lotto en Español – En la clase

© *Colette Elliott, Belén de Vicente Fisher and Brilliant Publications Limited.*
This board may be photocopied for use by the purchaser.

¡Lotto! (Tablero 2)   Nombre: _____

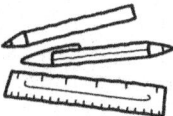

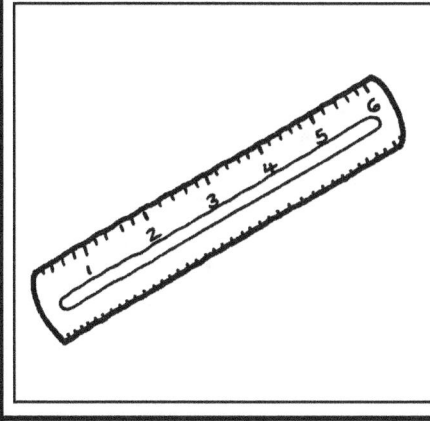  

  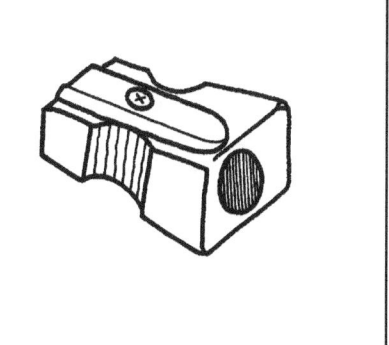

Lotto en Español – En la clase

© *Colette Elliott, Belén de Vicente Fisher and Brilliant Publications Limited.*
This board may be photocopied for use by the purchaser.

¡Lotto! (Tablero 3) Nombre: _____

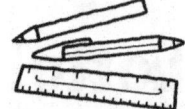

 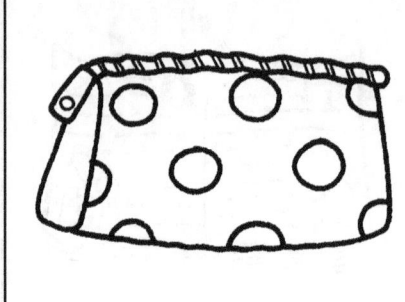 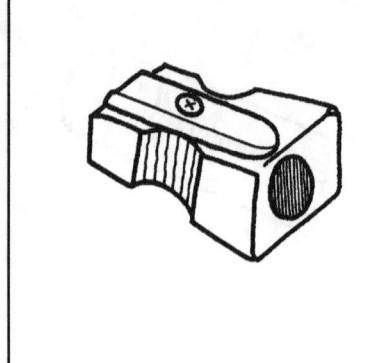

Lotto en Español – En la clase

© Colette Elliott, Belén de Vicente Fisher and Brilliant Publications Limited.
This board may be photocopied for use by the purchaser.

¡Lotto! (Tablero 4) Nombre: _____

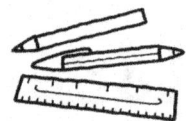

Lotto en Español – En la clase

© Colette Elliott, Belén de Vicente Fisher and Brilliant Publications Limited.
This board may be photocopied for use by the purchaser.

¡Lotto! (Tablero 1)   Nombre: _____

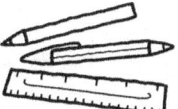

una barra de pegamento	un libro	una calculadora

una regla	una goma	unas tijeras

Lotto en Español – En la clase

¡Lotto! (Tablero 2)   Nombre: _____

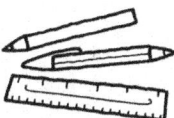

una regla	unas tijeras	un bolígrafo
		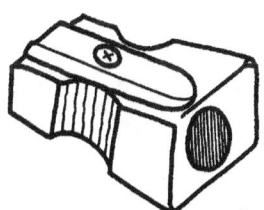
una barra de pegamento	un estuche	un sacapuntas

Lotto en Español – En la clase

¡Lotto! (Tablero 3)   Nombre: _____

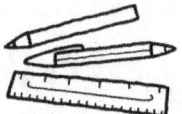

	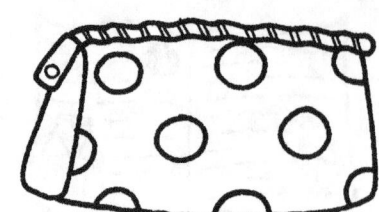	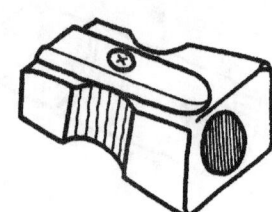
una mochila	un estuche	un sacapuntas
		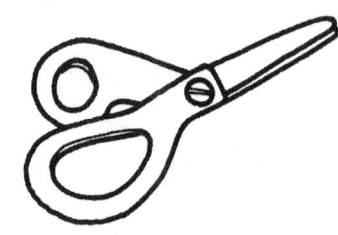
una goma	un cuaderno	unas tijeras

¡Lotto! (Tablero 4)   Nombre: _____

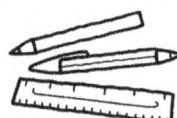

un cuaderno	un libro	un bolígrafo

unas tijeras	un lápiz	una mochila

¡Lotto! (Tablero 1)   Nombre: _____

una barra de pegamento	un libro	una calculadora
una regla	una goma	unas tijeras

Lotto en Español – En la clase

¡Lotto! (Tablero 2)   Nombre: _____

una regla	unas tijeras	un bolígrafo
una barra de pegamento	un estuche	un sacapuntas

Lotto en Español – En la clase

¡Lotto! (Tablero 3) Nombre: _____

una mochila	un estuche	un sacapuntas
una goma	un cuaderno	unas tijeras

¡Lotto! (Tablero 4) Nombre: _____

un cuaderno	un libro	un bolígrafo
unas tijeras	un lápiz	una mochila

La ropa

Team 1 to win	Start on 2 or 7
Team 2 to win	Start on 1, 3, 4 or 12
Team 3 to win	Start on 3, 5, 7, 10 or 11
Team 4 to win	Start on 5, 7, 8 or 9
All teams to win	Start on 6

These numbers refer to the numbers on the left and right of the grid below.

Tick the white boxes in the grid as you call out the words.

					Winning team										
				2	1	2&3	2	3&4	All	1,3,4	4	4	3	3	2	
Order of call	1	unos zapatos	some shoes													1
	2	un jersey	a jumper													2
	3	un vestido	a dress													3
	4	unos pantalones	a pair of trousers													4
	5	unos vaqueros	a pair of jeans													5
	6	una camiseta	a T-shirt													6
	7	un sombrero	a hat													7
	8	una falda	a skirt													8
	9	una camisa	a shirt													9
	10	una corbata	a tie													10
	11	unos calcetines	some socks													11
	12	unos pantalones cortos	a pair of shorts													12
	1	unos zapatos	some shoes													1
	2	un jersey	a jumper													2
	3	un vestido	a dress													3
	4	unos pantalones	a pair of trousers													4
	5	unos vaqueros	a pair of jeans													5
	6	una camiseta	a T-shirt													6
	7	un sombrero	a hat													7
	8	una falda	a skirt													8
	9	una camisa	a shirt													9

Lotto en Español

¡Lotto! (Tablero 1)   Nombre: _____

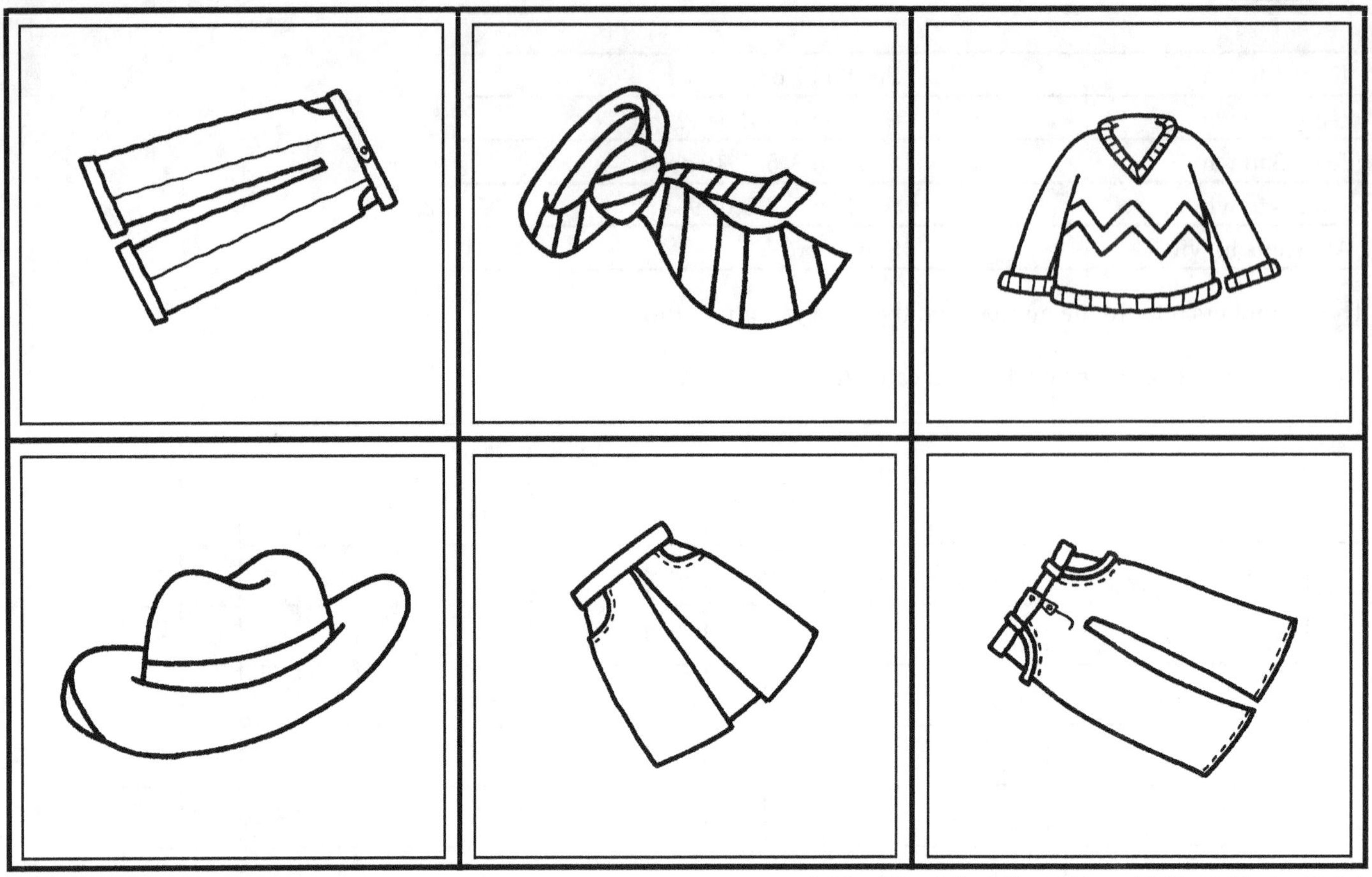

Lotto en Español – La ropa

© Colette Elliott, Belén de Vicente Fisher and Brilliant Publications Limited.
This board may be photocopied for use by the purchaser.

¡Lotto! (Tablero 2)   Nombre: _____

Lotto en Español – La ropa

© Colette Elliott, Belén de Vicente Fisher and Brilliant Publications Limited.
This board may be photocopied for use by the purchaser.

¡Lotto! (Tablero 3) Nombre: _____

Lotto en Español – La ropa   © *Colette Elliott, Belén de Vicente Fisher and Brilliant Publications Limited.*
This board may be photocopied for use by the purchaser.

¡Lotto! (Tablero 4) Nombre: _____

¡Lotto! (Tablero 1)   Nombre: _____

 unos pantalones	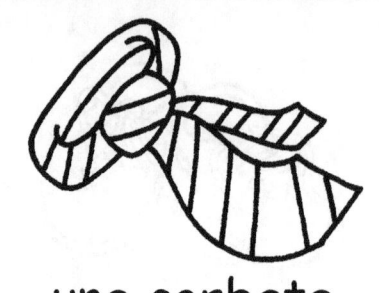 una corbata	 un jersey
 un sombrero	 una falda	 unos vaqueros

Lotto en Español – La ropa

© Colette Elliott, Belén de Vicente Fisher and Brilliant Publications Limited.
This board may be photocopied for use by the purchaser.

¡Lotto! (Tablero 2)   Nombre: _____

 una falda	 unos zapatos	 una camisa
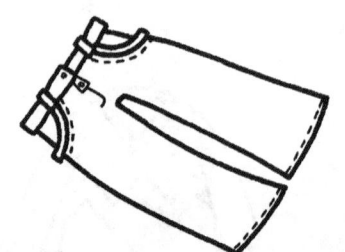 unos vaqueros	 una camiseta	 unos pantalones

Lotto en Español – La ropa

© Colette Elliott, Belén de Vicente Fisher and Brilliant Publications Limited.
This board may be photocopied for use by the purchaser.

¡Lotto! (Tablero 3)   Nombre: _____

 unos pantalones cortos	 unos zapatos	 unos calcetines
 un vestido	 un sombrero	 unos vaqueros

Lotto en Español – La ropa

¡Lotto! (Tablero 4)   Nombre: _____

 un vestido	 unos vaqueros	 una camisa
 unos pantalones cortos	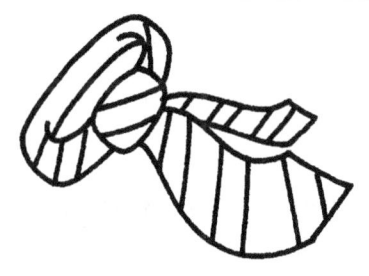 una corbata	 un jersey

¡Lotto! (Tablero 1)   Nombre: _____

unos pantalones	una corbata	un jersey
un sombrero	una falda	unos vaqueros

Lotto en Español – La ropa

© Colette Elliott, Belén de Vicente Fisher and Brilliant Publications Limited.
This board may be photocopied for use by the purchaser.

¡Lotto! (Tablero 2)   Nombre: _____

una falda	unos zapatos	una camisa
unos vaqueros	una camiseta	unos pantalones

Lotto en Español – La ropa

© Colette Elliott, Belén de Vicente Fisher and Brilliant Publications Limited.
This board may be photocopied for use by the purchaser.

¡Lotto! (Tablero 3)   Nombre: _____

unos pantalones cortos	unos zapatos	unos calcetines
un vestido	un sombrero	unos vaqueros

¡Lotto! (Tablero 4)   Nombre: _____

un vestido	unos vaqueros	una camisa
unos pantalones cortos	una corbata	un jersey

La Navidad

Team 1 to win	Start on 2 or 7
Team 2 to win	Start on 1, 3, 4 or 12
Team 3 to win	Start on 3, 5, 7, 10 or 11
Team 4 to win	Start on 5, 7, 8 or 9
All teams to win	Start on 6

These numbers refer to the numbers on the left and right of the grid below.

Tick the white boxes in the grid as you call out the words.

					Winning team										
					2	1	2&3	2	3&4	All	1,3,4	4	4	3	3	2	
Order of call	1	el acebo	holly													1
	2	el pavo	the turkey													2
	3	Papá Noel	Father Christmas													3
	4	el muñeco de nieve	the snowman													4
	5	Feliz Navidad	Happy Christmas!													5
	6	el árbol de Navidad	the Christmas tree													6
	7	el 25 de diciembre	25th December													7
	8	la estrella	the star													8
	9	los regalos	the presents													9
	10	el belén	the crib													10
	11	la vela	the candle													11
	12	el reno	a reindeer													12
	1	el acebo	holly													1
	2	el pavo	the turkey													2
	3	Papá Noel	Father Christmas													3
	4	el muñeco de nieve	the snowman													4
	5	Feliz Navidad	Happy Christmas													5
	6	el árbol de Navidad	the Christmas tree													6
	7	el 25 de diciembre	25th December													7
	8	la estrella	the star													8
	9	los regalos	the presents													9

We have used the definite article (el/la) for the Christmas words (instead of the indefinite article as used for other topics) as it seemed more appropriate. This could provide the stimulus for getting children to practise both forms.

¡Lotto! (Tablero 1) Nombre: _____

Lotto en Español – La Navidad

¡Lotto! (Tablero 2) Nombre: _____

 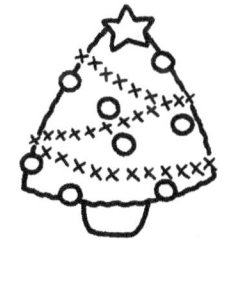 

Lotto en Español – La Navidad

¡Lotto! (Tablero 3) Nombre: _____

Lotto en Español – La Navidad

¡Lotto! (Tablero 4) Nombre: _____

¡Lotto! (Tablero 1)   Nombre: _____

el muñeco de nieve	el belén	el pavo

el 25 de diciembre	la estrella	Feliz Navidad

Lotto en Español – La Navidad

© Colette Elliott, Belén de Vicente Fisher and Brilliant Publications Limited.
This board may be photocopied for use by the purchaser.

¡Lotto! (Tablero 2)   Nombre: _____

la estrella	el acebo	los regalos

Feliz Navidad	el árbol de Navidad	el muñeco de nieve

Lotto en Español – La Navidad

© Colette Elliott, Belén de Vicente Fisher and Brilliant Publications Limited.
This board may be photocopied for use by the purchaser.

¡Lotto! (Tablero 3)   Nombre: _____

el reno	el acebo	la vela

Papá Noel	el 25 de diciembre	Feliz Navidad

Lotto en Español – La Navidad

© Colette Elliott, Belén de Vicente Fisher and Brilliant Publications Limited.
This board may be photocopied for use by the purchaser.

¡Lotto! (Tablero 4)   Nombre: _____

Papá Noel	Feliz Navidad	los regalos

el reno	el belén	el pavo

Lotto en Español – La Navidad

© Colette Elliott, Belén de Vicente Fisher and Brilliant Publications Limited.
This board may be photocopied for use by the purchaser.

¡Lotto! (Tablero 1) Nombre: _____

el muñeco de nieve	el belén	el pavo
el 25 de diciembre	la estrella	Feliz Navidad

Lotto en Español – La Navidad

¡Lotto! (Tablero 2) Nombre: _____

la estrella	el acebo	los regalos
Feliz Navidad	el árbol de Navidad	el muñeco de nieve

Lotto en Español – La Navidad

¡Lotto! (Tablero 3)   Nombre: _____

el reno	el acebo	la vela
Papá Noel	el 25 de diciembre	Feliz Navidad

Lotto en Español – La Navidad

© Colette Elliott, Belén de Vicente Fisher and Brilliant Publications Limited.
This board may be photocopied for use by the purchaser.

¡Lotto! (Tablero 4)   Nombre: _____

Papá Noel	Feliz Navidad	los regalos
el reno	el belén	el pavo

¡Lotto! (Tablero   )   Nombre: _____

Lotto en Español

¡Lotto! (Tablero   )   Nombre: _____

List of vocabulary used in the games

Los números del 1 al 12
uno	1
dos	2
tres	3
cuatro	4
cinco	5
seis	6
siete	7
ocho	8
nueve	9
diez	10
once	11
doce	12

Los números del 1 al 60
siete	7
doce	12
quince	15
diecinueve	19
veintiséis	26
treinta y cuatro	34
treinta y cinco	35
cuarenta y uno	41
cuarenta y dos	42
cincuenta	50
cincuenta y ocho	58
sesenta	60

Los animales
un pato	a duck
un gato	a cat
un caballo	a horse
un perro	a dog
un cerdo	a pig
una cobaya	a Guinea pig
un hámster	a hamster
un conejo	a rabbit
un pez	a goldfish
una gallina	a hen
un ratón	a mouse
una vaca	a cow

¡Que aproveche!
unos caramelos	some sweets
unas patatas fritas	some chips
un poco de queso	some cheese
una tarta	a cake
un helado	an ice-cream
un huevo	an egg
un poco de pan	some bread
un pollo	a chicken
una manzana	an apple
un jamón	some ham
una patata	a potato
un brik de leche	a carton of milk

En la clase
una barra de pegamento	a glue stick
un cuaderno	a workbook
una calculadora	a calculator
una mochila	a school bag
unas tijeras	some scissors
un lápiz	a pencil
una goma	a rubber
un libro	a book
una regla	a ruler
un bolígrafo	a pen
un sacapuntas	a pencil sharpener
un estuche	a pencil case

La ropa
un sombrero	a hat
unos calcetines	some socks
unos zapatos	some shoes
una camisa	a shirt
una corbata	a tie
unos vaqueros	a pair of jeans
un vestido	a dress
unos pantalones	a pair of trousers
un jersey	a jumper
una falda	a skirt
unos pantalones cortos	a pair of shorts
una camiseta	a T-shirt

La Navidad
el acebo	holly
el pavo	the turkey
Papá Noel	Father Christmas
Feliz Navidad	Happy Christmas
el árbol de Navidad	the Christmas tree
el 25 de diciembre	25th December
la estrella	the star
los regalos	the presents
el belén	the crib
la vela	the candle
el reno	the reindeer
el muñeco de nieve	the snowman

Ages: 7–11 yrs

Juguemos Todos Juntos
20 Games to Play with Children to Encourage and Reinforce Spanish Language and Vocabulary

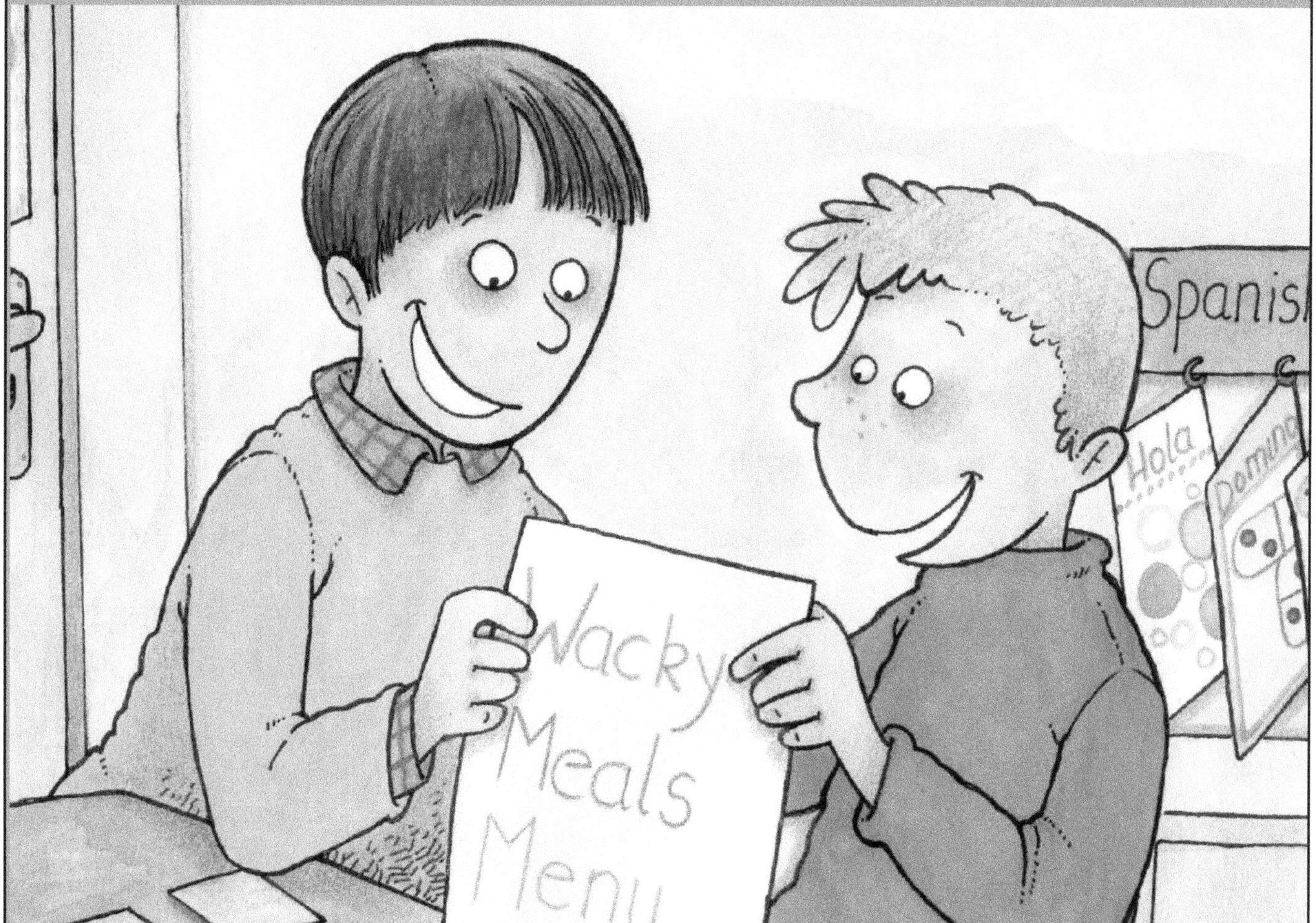

Kathy Williams and
Beatriz Rubio

Juguemos Todos Juntos

20 Games to Play with Children to Encourage and Reinforce Spanish Language and Vocabulary

Kathy Williams and
Beatriz Rubio

We hope you and your pupils enjoy playing the games in this book. Brilliant Publications publishes many other books for teaching modern foreign languages. To find out more details on any of the titles listed below, please go to our website: www.brilliantpublications.co.uk.

100+ Fun Ideas for Practising Modern Foreign Languages in the Primary Classroom	978-1-903853-98-6
More Fun Ideas for Advancing Modern Foreign Language Learners in the Primary Classroom	978-1-905780-72-3
¡Es Español!	978-1-903853-64-1
¡Vamos a Cantar!	978-1-905780-13-6
Spanish Pen Pals Made Easy	978-1-905780-42-6
Lotto en Español	978-1-905780-47-1
Spanish Festivals and Traditions	978-1-905780-53-2
Buena Idea	978-1-905780-63-1
Chantez Plus Fort!	978-1-903853-37-5
Hexagonie Part 1	978-1-905780-59-4
Hexagonie Part 2	978-1-905780-18-1
Jouons Tous Ensemble	978-1-903853-81-8
C'est Français!	978-1-903853-02-3
J'aime Chanter!	978-1-905780-11-2
J'aime Parler!	978-1-905780-12-9
French Pen Pals Made Easy	978-1-905780-10-5
Loto Français	978-1-905780-45-7
French Festivals and Traditions	978-1-905780-44-0
Bonne Idée	978-1-905780-62-4
Unforgettable French	978-1-78317-093-7
Das ist Deutsch	978-1-905780-15-0
Wir Spielen Zusammen	978-1-903853-97-9
German Pen Pals Made Easy	978-1-905780-43-3
Deutsch-Lotto	978-1-905780-46-4
German Festivals and Traditions	978-1-905780-52-5
Gute Idee	978-1-905780-65-5
Giochiamo Tutti Insieme	978-1-903853-96-2
Lotto in Italiano	978-1-905780-48-8
Buon'Idea	978-0-85747-696-8

Published by Brilliant Publications Limited
Unit 10
Sparrow Hall Farm
Edlesborough
Dunstable
Bedfordshire
LU6 2ES, UK

Website: www.brilliantpublications.co.uk

General information enquiries:
Tel: 01525 222292

The name Brilliant Publications and the logo are registered trademarks.

Written by Kathy Williams and Beatriz Rubio
Cover and inside illustrations by Chantal Kees
© Kathy Williams and Beatriz Rubio 2006

Printed ISBN: 978-1-903853-95-5
ebook ISBN: 978-0-85747-123-9

First published and printed in the UK 2006. Reprinted 2007 and 2010.
10 9 8 7 6 5 4 3

The right of Kathy Williams and Beatriz Rubio to be identified as the authors of this work has been asserted by themselves in accordance with the Copyright, Designs and Patents Act 1988.

Pages 10, 12–13, 15–17, 20, 22, 24, 26–28, 30–31, 33–34, 36–37, 39, 41–42, 44, 47–48, 50 and 52 may be photocopied by the purchasing institution or individual teachers for classroom use only, without permission from the publisher and without declaration to the Copyright Licensing Agency or Publishers' Licensing Services. No other part of this book may be reproduced in any other form or for any other purpose, without the prior permission of the publisher.

Contents

All the games involve speaking, and most can be adapted to practise alternative language. See individual game descriptions for ideas.

	Language focus	Page
Introduction		4

Games involving speech and action

Hola ball game	introductions	5
Colour relay	colours	6
Slap down numbers	numbers	7
Calling all animals	animals	8

Games particularly involving writing/spelling

Domino months	months	9–10
Write back	numbers	11–13
Rhyming pairs	familiar words	14–17
Spelling snake	any language	18–20
Sort yourself out	familiar words	21–22
Silly sentences	familiar words	23–24

Games involving cards/boards and speech/writing

Wacky meals	food	25–28
House designers	rooms	29–31
Super sporty week	sports/days	32–34
Weather reporters	weather	35–37
Triple time	time	38–39
The best/worst day ever at school	school subjects/time	40–42
Like it or not	likes and dislikes	43–44
A tour of Spain	transport/places in Spain	45–48
Quiz corners	any language	49–50
Rock, paper, scissors	any language	51–52

Introduction

The games in this book are designed to complement language teaching and learning, either in the classroom or at home. They are fun to play, and there is no age limit – children and adults alike can enjoy the different types of games.

Each game concentrates on one or two specific language areas. Many of the games can be adapted to practise other language vocabulary as appropriate.

All the games encourage speaking and listening. The skills of reading and writing are emphasized to different degrees in the different games.

The instructions for each game set out:
- the objectives for the game
- how to set it up
- how to play it
- extensions/variations

Some of the games require cards and boards and these are provided as photocopiable resource pages. It is a good idea to allow some time to prepare the items needed for each game before introducing them into play. If the playing cards and boards are photocopied onto thin card and laminated, you will be able to use them again and again for many years.

Hola ball game

Action game

Objectives
- To practise key introduction words
- Game can be extended to include other introduction phrases as required

Vocabulario – Key words
hola	hello
adiós	goodbye
¿cómo estás?	how are you?
bien, gracias	I'm fine, thank you
me llamo …	my name is …

Setting up the game
- You need two or more different coloured balls.

How to play the game

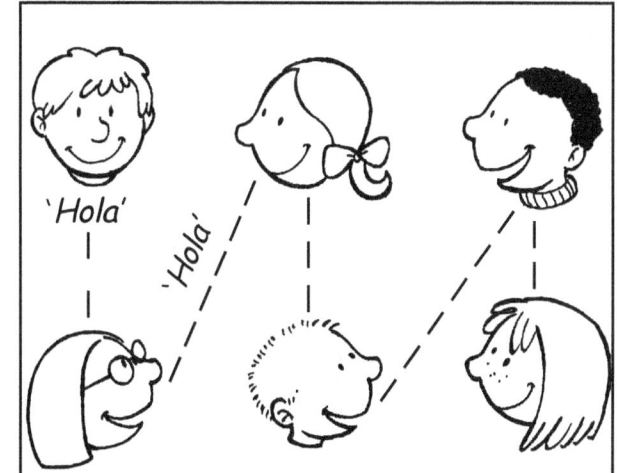

1. Pupils stand in two lines facing each other. The end pupil starts with one of the balls, and throws it to the pupil opposite. That person then throws the ball to the pupil diagonally opposite, who throws it this time to the person directly opposite and so on. The ball thus makes its way in a zig-zag along the two lines.
2. While throwing and catching the ball, each pupil must say 'Hola'. Using a different coloured ball, repeat the game, but this time say 'Adiós'.
3. Now, tell the children to take note of the colour of the ball. Using the red ball, for instance, they say 'Hola', and with the blue ball, they say 'Adiós'.
4. Start the game off with one ball again, then introduce the other ball after a couple of throws. This makes them think about which word they are saying! You could introduce further coloured balls with '¿Cómo estás?', 'Bien, gracias', 'Me llamo …'. Try as many as the group can manage!
5. As a rounding-up test, stand in a large circle, and pick a pupil to hold the coloured balls in the centre. They then throw the balls (gently!) to pupils at random who must say the appropriate phrase for that colour of ball as it is thrown. Younger pupils may find that concentrating on more than two colours/phrases at once is too difficult, but older groups will enjoy the challenge of several colours/phrases in this game.

Extensions/variations
- Adapt the game to practise vocabulary groups; each time a player catches the ball the pupil must say a different animal word/colour/food item.
- Use the ball throwing idea to practise lists of words, passing the ball up and down the line or in a circle; practise the alphabet in Spanish/days/months/numbers.

© Kathy Williams and Beatriz Rubio

Colour relay

Action game

Objective
- To practise saying colour words and respond by picking up the correct colour from a choice

Vocabulario – Key words

rojo	red
blanco	white
azul	blue
negro	black
verde	green
rosa	pink
amarillo	yellow
marrón	brown
naranja	orange
gris	grey

Setting up the game
- Pupils play in teams.
- You will need several items of different colours, the same number of items for each team.
- The game is best played in a large space so that the participants can run back and forth.

How to play the game

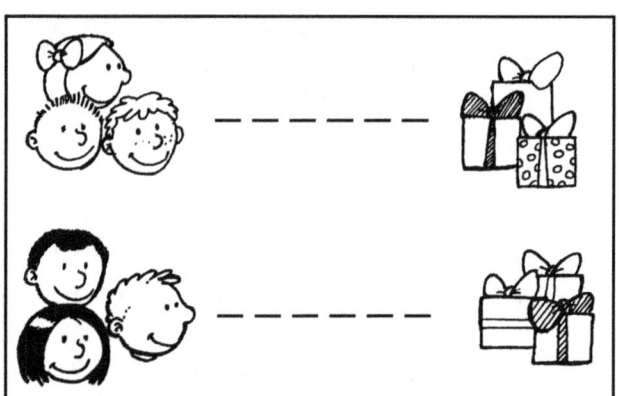

1. Place sets of coloured items in piles at one end of the room (or space you are playing in).
2. The teams line up opposite the coloured items so that they can race against each other in a back-and-forth relay.
3. The teacher calls out the first colour to start the race.
4. The first team member from each team runs to collect that coloured item from their team pile, and returns to the team.
5. On their return they say another colour (in Spanish) to be picked up. The next player runs to collect that coloured item, returns to the rest of the team and says the next colour to be picked up.
6. The game continues in this way, with players joining the back of the line on their return to the team, storing all the items at the back of the line, until all the coloured items have been collected.
7. The winning team is the one that successfully collects all the items first. It is a good idea to have three or four small teams, with extra helpers to monitor the teams, so that everyone gets more than one turn, and you can listen carefully to the players saying the colours in SPANISH. You could have a rule that anyone heard saying the wrong colour, or not using Spanish, has to run back and forth again (without picking up another item) before the next player has a turn.

Extension/variation
- To make the game more challenging pupils could say two or three colours at once, with plenty of items in the pile to choose from.

Juguemos Todos Juntos

© Kathy Williams and Beatriz Rubio

Slap down numbers

Action game

Objectives
- To practise saying the numbers one to ten
- To listen carefully
- To respond quickly to recognition of numbers in Spanish

Vocabulario – Key words
uno	one
dos	two
tres	three
cuatro	four
cinco	five
seis	six
siete	seven
ocho	eight
nueve	nine
diez	ten

Setting up the game
- Players are in pairs, sitting at a table, or where they can put their hands down quickly onto a flat surface.

How to play the game
1. Toss a coin to decide who starts. Both players have their hands on their heads to begin the game.
2. Choose one player to start first. Both players count together in Spanish, slowly.
3. When the counting reaches the number that player one has decided to stop at, he slaps his hands down, and spreads out the appropriate number of fingers on the table. For example the counting goes: 'uno … dos … tres …' but on 'cuatro' he slaps his hand down showing four fingers. Encourage the children to use both hands.
4. Player two must respond as quickly as possible by putting her hands down too, BUT she too must only put down the correct number of fingers, i.e. in this case only four.
5. If she puts the correct number of fingers down, then she becomes the caller. If she is not correct then player one continues to make the number choices.

Extension/variation
- The game can be made more challenging by counting up in twos, by counting backwards or by counting very quickly.

Calling all animals

Action game

Objective
- To practise saying animal words

Vocabulario – Key words

gato (m)	cat
ratón (m)	mouse
perro (m)	dog
araña (f)	spider
caballo (m)	horse
rana (f)	frog
conejo (m)	rabbit
pez (m)	fish
pájaro (m)	bird
conejillo de Indias (m)	guinea-pig

Setting up the game
- Any number of pupils can play. Each player can have a different animal name given to them if there are 10 or less players; if there are more players the animal words can be used more than once.
- You need enough space for the group to form a circle.

How to play the game
1. The group forms a circle and one pupil is chosen at random to be 'it', in the middle of the circle.
2. All the animal words should be introduced and practised first so that everyone is familiar with the words.
3. Each player is then given an animal name. The whole group hears the names being given out and they can all practise each word as it is introduced. Make sure that everyone knows exactly how to say what they are, and that the person in the middle can say all the animal words (some reminding might be needed).
4. The player who is 'it' decides on an animal name to say and says it aloud three times in succession.
5. The aim of the game is for the person who has been given that animal name to join in and say their name once but before the 'it' person has finished saying it three times! If the 'animal' succeeds, he/she is then 'it' instead. If the 'it' person manages to say the word three times before the person with that animal name has said his name once, the player in the middle stays as 'it'. Everyone who manages to be 'it' must aim to stay there as long as possible, and all the others must try to get him/her out.
6. If the circle players cannot join in before their names are said three times, adjust to saying the name five times (sometimes needed for younger children).

Extensions/variations
- This game is very adaptable as it can be played with any vocabulary that you wish to practise, e.g. buildings, food, parts of the body. It works well with Spanish girls'/boys' names.
- Another way to play is for you to spell the animal word out, either in Spanish or English. The player who thinks that the animal name is theirs has to run around the outside of the circle back to their place before you finish spelling the word (do it slowly to give them a chance!), and say the word to make sure they were right to run.

Domino months

Spelling game

Objective
- To practise the months in Spanish with particular emphasis on word recognition in writing

Setting up the game
- Pupils can either play in pairs or groups with one set of dominoes (page 10) per pair.
- The dominoes could be coloured, decorated, and laminated and/or mounted on card before use.

Vocabulario – Key words
enero	January
febrero	February
marzo	March
abril	April
mayo	May
junio	June
julio	July
agosto	August
septiembre	September
octubre	October
noviembre	November
diciembre	December

How to play the game
1. Place the dominoes face down in front of the players with one domino upturned to start the game. The aim of the game is to match the dominoes to make complete month words.
2. Players each take five dominoes at random and look at them without revealing them to their opponent(s). The rest of the dominoes are put in a pile on the table.
3. One player takes a turn first, trying to complete a month word by placing one of his dominoes before or after the starting domino. Dominoes can be placed at right angles so the words do not have to go in one continuous straight line. If the first player cannot go, the other player(s) take their turn. If none of the players can place a domino, then the first player picks one up from the pile and plays the card if it completes a domino month. Play continues with players either putting down a domino or picking one up from the pile.
4. The winner is the player who uses up all of their dominoes first, or who has the least number of cards left. It isn't always possible to carry on until all the dominoes have been put down. In the case of a tie-break, maybe add the number of letters on each card together, the person with the least being the winner!
5. You will need to monitor correct positioning of the dominoes to ensure correct word completion. Saying the names of the months out loud as they are completed helps to link the written and spoken words.

Domino months

Enlarge photocopy at 115% onto thin card and cut out.

bre	noviem	bre	ju	bre	ju
bre	diciem	lio	octu	ro	septiem
bre	a	bril	mar	nio	febre
ro	ma	yo	ju	sto	ene
ro	febre	nio	octu	ro	ju
zo	ene	zo	ene	sto	mar
ro	ago	lio	ago	lio	ju

This page may be photocopied for use by the purchasing institution only.

Juguemos Todos Juntos

Write back

Spelling game

Objectives
- To reinforce knowledge of numbers up to twenty
- Version 1 practises recognition of number words. Version 2 reinforces the spellings of the numbers

Setting up the game
- Pupils play in pairs using one of the grids from number sheet (page 12) per pair, or one customized in advance to practise specific numbers or words (page 13).
- The children will need some counters or coins.

Vocabulario – Key words

uno	one
dos	two
tres	three
cuatro	four
cinco	five
seis	six
siete	seven
ocho	eight
nueve	nine
diez	ten
once	eleven
doce	twelve
trece	thirteen
catorce	fourteen
quince	fifteen
dieciséis	sixteen
diecisiete	seventeen
dieciocho	eighteen
diecinueve	nineteen
veinte	twenty

How to play the game

Version 1
1. The players have a number grid in front of them. Depending on their skill, this can be either A, B or C (from page 12) or one you have custom made using page 13.
2. Player one looks at the grid, decides on a number, but does not tell their partner. Using a finger, player one gently taps out that amount on their partner's back.
3. The partner then places a counter on the correct number on the grid and recites the number in Spanish.
4. The game continues with each player taking turns until all the numbers are covered.

Version 2
1. The players have a grid as in version 1, but instead of tapping the required number of times for their partner to recognize, they must slowly spell out the word on their partner's back. It is best to 'draw' one letter at a time, rather than write the whole word in joined-up writing. However, the whole word technique works well with older or more able pupils.
2. As before, the player on whose back the word is written must place their counter on the correct word on the grid, saying it in Spanish.

Extension/variation
- This game can be adapted to reinforce spellings in any language area using the blank grid to set out the language to be practised. Alternatively, the 'receiving' player writes down what they think has been spelled on their back onto a blank grid.

© Kathy Williams and Beatriz Rubio

Juguemos Todos Juntos

www.brilliantpublications.co.uk

Write back number grid

Photocopy one grid per pair (can use either Grid A, B or C)

Grid A

uno	dos	tres	cuatro	cinco
seis	siete	ocho	nueve	diez

Grid B

uno	dos	tres	cuatro	cinco
seis	siete	ocho	nueve	diez
once	doce	trece	catorce	quince
dieciséis	diecisiete	dieciocho	diecinueve	veinte

Grid C

once	doce	trece	catorce	quince
dieciséis	diecisiete	dieciocho	diecinueve	veinte

This page may be photocopied for use by the purchasing institution only.

Juguemos Todos Juntos © Kathy Williams and Beatriz Rubio

Write back blank number grid

Use this to prepare the language that you want to practise, or use the grid to write your answers in.

Grid A

Grid B

Grid C

Rhyming pairs

Spelling game

Objectives
- To facilitate close examination of familiar words in their written form
- To introduce the concept of using word endings to help identify word gender (words used here are both masculine and feminine; words ending in 'a' are generally feminine, and those ending in 'o' masculine)
- Saying the words out loud links the spelling patterns with pronunciation. Looking at the last syllable(s) to find rhyming pairs reinforces their spelling and pronunciation

Vocabulario – Key words
rat**ón** (m)	mouse
bot**ón** (m)	button
ingl**és**	English
franc**és**	French
ro**dilla** (f)	knee
tor**tilla** (f)	Spanish omelette
m**adre** (f)	mother
p**adre** (m)	father
jar**dín** (m)	garden
co**jín** (f)	cushion
sombr**ero** (m)	hat
tor**ero** (m)	bullfighter
abr**igo** (m)	coat
am**igo** (m)	friend
ar**aña** (f)	spider
mont**aña** (f)	mountain
come**dor** (m)	dining room
ordena**dor** (m)	computer

Setting up the game
- You need to photocopy and cut out the rhyme cards (pages 15–16).
- The children will need some counters or coins.
- Players play in groups of three. Each pupil will need to pick a picture board from the selection (pages 16–17).

How to play the game
1. All the cards are placed face down and spread out on the table in front of the players.
2. The game is played as a matching pictures pairs game, only this time the matching pairs are rhyming written words.
3. Players must take turns to turn over two cards at random.
4. If they have a rhyming pair they say the two words.
5. If the pair does not rhyme they turn the cards back over and try to remember for next time where each card is.
6. When a player finds a matching pair he/she looks to see if the pair is pictured on their board.
7. If it is, they place counters or coins on the appropriate pictures and put the cards to one side. If the cards aren't pictured, he/she puts them back in the middle of the table, face down.
8. The winner is the player who completes their board first.

Extension/variation
- Players could play the game using boards and words they have created themselves. They could use vocabulary they already know (chosen either individually or as a group) or use dictionaries to look up new words.

Rhyming pairs game cards

ratón	botón
francés	inglés
rodilla	tortilla
jardín	cojín
madre	padre
sombrero	torero

Rhyming pairs game cards

abrigo	amigo
araña	montaña
comedor	ordenador

	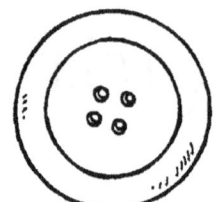
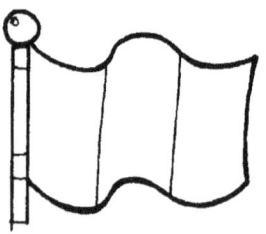	
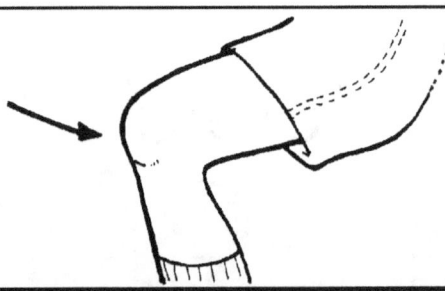	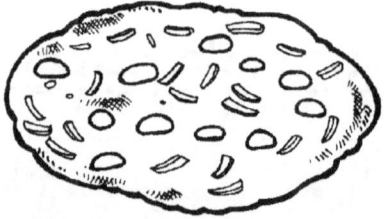

This page may be photocopied for use by the purchasing institution only.

Juguemos Todos Juntos

Rhyming pairs board

This page may be photocopied for use by the purchasing institution only.

Juguemos Todos Juntos

Spelling snake

Spelling game

Objective
- To encourage the use of a specific area of vocabulary or to give players the opportunity to use any language that they know

Setting up the game
- This game can be played with four or more people.
- Each child needs a blank copy of the 'spelling snake' (page 20).

How to play the game
1. Start as a whole group and brainstorm a large number of words within a vocabulary area, or several areas. At the end of this session, write these words, correctly spelled onto the board, or provide a prepared list that contains the words you elicited from the players. (This list would benefit from containing words that start or finish with a variety of letters – take care that not all your words end in the letter 'o' for example).
2. Give the players a couple of minutes to study the words, then remove them from view.
3. Each player writes one word of their choice from the target list into the first section of their spelling snake (see 'Comienza aquí').
4. All players then simultaneously pass the snake on to another player, and here you must ensure random exchanges.
5. Using the final letter of the first word, each player must then write in a new word from the list, and then pass the snake on as before.
6. If a player cannot write a word starting with the last letter (which is often not possible), he/she writes a new word that is unconnected and passes on the snake as before.
7. The class continue to write on and pass around the snakes until all the spaces are full. You can make the game easier by allowing repeats of the same word, or harder by having a 'no repeats' rule.
8. When the snakes are complete, and there may be some which take longer than others, the snake that each player ends with becomes the one which will score or lose them points.

To score points

- Ask each player to check the words on his snake against the original list. A correctly spelled word gets 2 points. Add on an extra 1 point for every word that starts with the last letter of the previous one. The winner is the player with the highest total of points at the end.
- If you tell the players how the scoring works before they start to play it will encourage everyone to spell correctly as they do not know which snake they will have at the end.

Extensions/variations

- Alternatively, tell the players that they are going to be able to use any words they like during the game, but that spelling must be correct. In this case play the game and then include a follow-up session to go over the words and their spellings together.
- If players do not have time to study the words immediately before the game, this game can be used to test spelling knowledge of a preset group of words.

Spelling snake

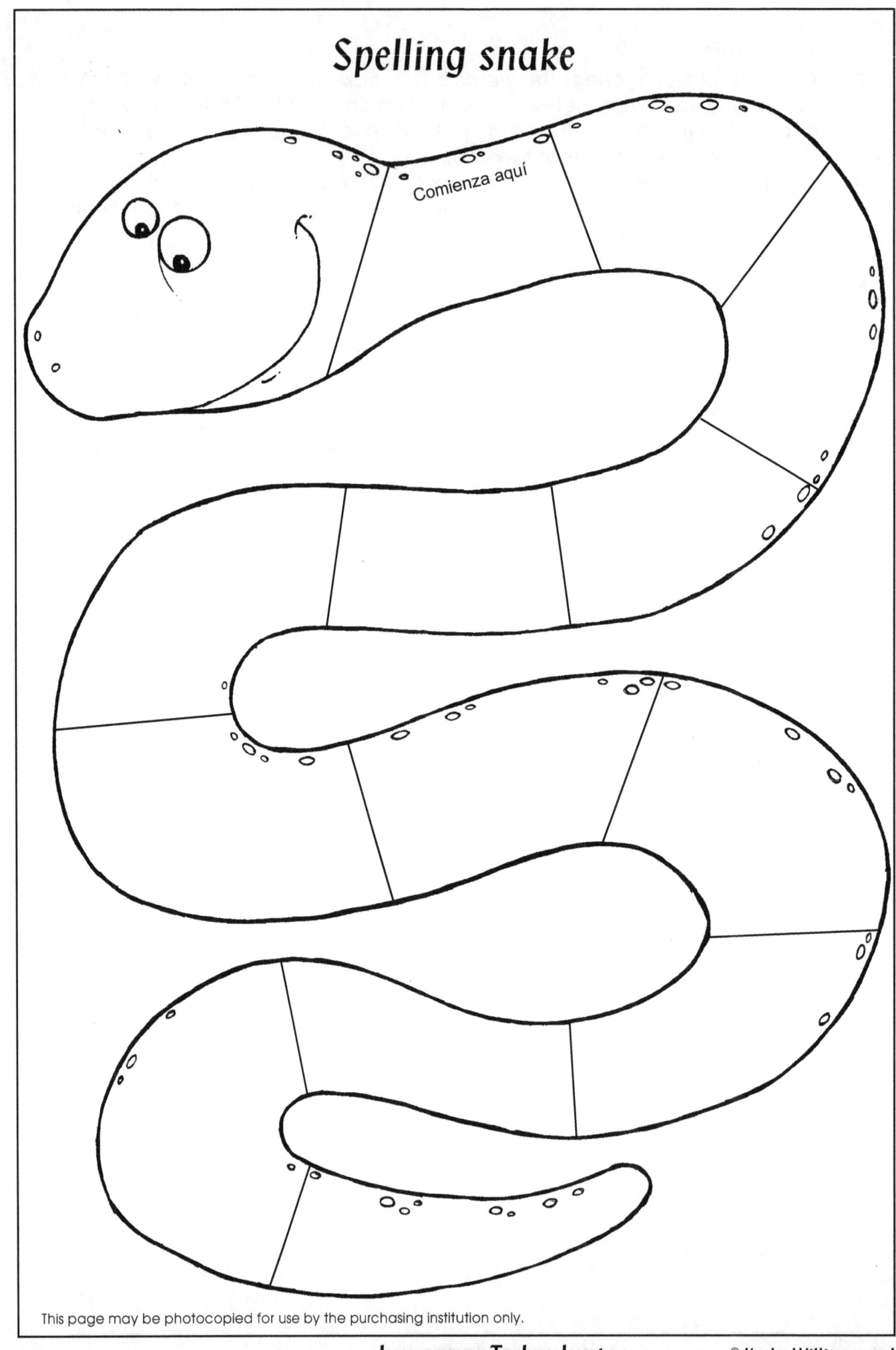

Comienza aquí

Sort yourself out

Spelling game

Objective
- To arrange sets of words beginning with the same letter into alphabetical order

Setting up the game
- You need 'sort yourself out' list of words (page 22) and blank sheets for the children's answers.
- Children will need some scissors and some pens/pencils.
- Children play in pairs.

How to play the game
1. Cut the word lists into separate columns and give each pair of children one list.
2. The children cut the words out individually into strips and mix them up.
3. They then must try to put their words into alphabetical order. They write down the words and their meanings, guessing for those they don't know. You could set a time limit for this task.
4. At the end of the allotted time, the teacher reads out or writes down the correct alphabetical order for each list and the word meanings. Players get a point for every correct position in the list and a point for each correct meaning.

Extension/variation
- The game can be played again using a different set of words or you could create your own list. This game is very useful for checking the pupils' understanding of vocabulary practised.

Vocabulario – Key words

abeja (f)	bee
abrigo (m)	coat
abril	April
araña (f)	spider
armario (m)	cupboard
avión (m)	aeroplane
caballo (m)	horse
calcetines (m)	socks
cerezas (f)	cherries
color (m)	colour
comedor (m)	dining room
conejo (m)	rabbit
garaje (m)	garage
gato (m)	cat
goma (f)	eraser/rubber
grande	big
gris	grey
guitarra (f)	guitar
lápiz (m)	pencil
leche (f)	milk
libro (m)	book
lila	lilac
luna (f)	moon
lunes (m)	Monday
mano (f)	hand
martes (m)	Tuesday
montaña (f)	mountain
monumento (m)	monument
museo (m)	museum
música (f)	music
ratón (m)	mouse
rectángulo (m)	rectangle
regla (f)	ruler
reina (f)	queen
rojo	red
rosa (f)	rose, pink
salón (m)	lounge
sandalias (f)	sandals
silla (f)	chair
sofá (m)	sofa
sombrero (m)	hat
sótano (m)	cellar
té (m)	tea
televisión (f)	television
trece	thirteen
tren (m)	train
tres	three
tienda (f)	shop
vaso (m)	glass
verano (m)	summer
vestido (m)	dress
viernes (m)	Friday
violín (m)	violin
volcán (m)	volcano

Sort yourself out

abeja	caballo	garaje
abrigo	calcetines	gato
abril	cerezas	goma
araña	color	grande
armario	comedor	gris
avión	conejo	guitarra
lápiz	mano	ratón
leche	martes	rectángulo
libro	montaña	regla
lila	monumento	reina
luna	museo	rojo
lunes	música	rosa
salón	té	vaso
sandalias	televisión	verano
silla	trece	vestido
sofá	tren	viernes
sombrero	tres	violín
sótano	tienda	volcán

This page may be photocopied for use by the purchasing institution only.

Silly sentences

Spelling game

Objective
- To encourage recognition of sentence building rules and parts of speech

Setting up the game
- Prepare the game by photocopying and cutting out the word sections (page 24), one for every player or pair of players.

How to play the game
1. Give each player (or pair) a set of mixed-up word sections.
2. Discuss the parts of a sentence: noun (el nombre), verb (el verbo), adjective (el adjetivo). Point out that in Spanish the adjective usually follows the noun. Remind the pupils that the verbs presented here are from different conjugations. Revise with them the third person singular of those verbs before starting the game (llevar - lleva; comer - come; perseguir - persigue).
3. Demonstrate a sentence that makes sense, for example 'El bombero lleva un sombrero rojo.'
4. Ask the players to form as many sensible sentences as they can, by changing around the words. Look at and discuss the parts of speech and word order.
5. Ask the pupils to see what 'silly' sentences they can create. Remember that the 'silly' sentences should still be formed correctly, e.g. 'El perro come un sombrero delicioso.'

Vocabulario – Key words

el bombero	the fireman
el perro	the dog
el gato	the cat
lleva	he/she/it wears
come	he/she/it eats
persigue	he/she/it chases
un sombrero	a hat
un pastel	a cake
un globo	a balloon
delicioso	delicious
largo	long
rojo	red
verde	green
azul	blue

Extension/variation
- Players could draw pictures of their favourite sentences. Play a mime game, where a pupil has to mime what has been drawn and the other players have to guess the 'silly' sentence.

Silly sentences

| el bombero | lleva | un sombrero | rojo | y verde |

| el perro | come | un pastel | delicioso |

| el gato | persigue | un globo | largo | y azul |

Wacky meals

Card game

Objective
- To recognize and use some food words, as well as the correct words for the different meal times

Setting up the game
- Players are in pairs or small groups.
- Each group will need a set of food word cards (page 27) and a 'menú' (page 28).

How to play the game
1. Each group has a set of food cards face down in front of them.
2. One player picks up a card at random and places it face up in the first 'para desayunar' position on the menu, saying aloud what the food item is in Spanish.
3. The second player then picks up another card and places it on the next breakfast position, saying the food item in Spanish. Some strange breakfast choices may be beginning to appear!
4. Players continue until all the meals are set.
5. When finished they discuss together what meals have been created using the sentence structures: 'Para desayunar tomo …' And so on.
6. Each pair or group then presents the 'wacky meals' that they have on their menus to the rest of the class.

Vocabulario – Key words

para …	for …
comer	lunch (lit. 'have lunch')
desayunar	breakfast (lit. 'have breakfast')
cenar	dinner/supper (lit. 'have dinner/supper')
tomo …	I'm having …
una manzana	an apple
(el) pan	bread
(la) mantequilla	butter
un pastel	a cake
una pera	a pear
(el) queso	cheese
(el) chocolate	chocolate
(las) patatas	potatoes
(las) patatas fritas	chips
(el) pollo	chicken
(la) tortilla	omelette
(la) sopa	soup
una coca-cola	a coke
un bocadillo	a sandwich
(el) jamón	ham
un zumo de naranja	an orange juice
un agua mineral	a mineral water
(los) cereales	cereal

Extensions/variations
- The picture cards (page 26) can be used instead of the food word cards to prompt usage of food words.
- The game can be played as a whole class if the menu sheet is enlarged. Individuals take turns to choose cards and place them or write the food item onto the menu.
- Using the same concept, make cards showing different items of clothing, and instead of a menu sheet, use places/events to dress for, for example 'Para ir **de vacaciones** llevo … (To go **on holiday** I wear …); Para ir **a la escuela** llevo … (To go **to school** I wear …); Para ir **a una fiesta** llevo … (To go **to a party** I wear …).' See what funny outfits emerge!

Wacky meals picture cards

Wacky meals food word cards

una manzana	pan	mantequilla
un pastel	una pera	queso
chocolate	patatas	patatas fritas
pollo	tortilla	sopa
una coca-cola	un bocadillo	jamón
un zumo de naranja	un agua mineral	cereales

This page may be photocopied for use by the purchasing institution only.

Wacky meals menu sheet

Menu choices

1 Para desayunar	2	3
1 Para comer	**2**	**3**
1 Para cenar	**2**	**3**

This page may be photocopied for use by the purchasing institution only.

Juguemos Todos Juntos

House designers

Board/card game

Objectives
- To use the names for rooms in the house
- To communicate information about the layout of a house
- The use of 'aquí' (here), 'allí' (there) and 'está' (is) can also be reinforced

Vocabulario – Key words
aquí	here
allí	there
está	is
la cocina	the kitchen
el salón	the lounge
el dormitorio	the bedroom
el vestíbulo	the hall
el cuarto de baño	the bathroom
el garaje	the garage
el comedor	the dining room
el ático	the attic

Setting up the game
- Pupils play in teams of three, with the teams racing each other.
- Two 'house design sheets' (page 30) are needed per group. Room pictures (page 31) can be used for guidance.
- A spacious room/area (two rooms could be used) to separate two of the three players in each team, so that they cannot see the other player's sheet.

How to play the game
1. One pair of players (players two and three) has a 'house design sheet', a set of room pictures, and a pen/pencil, and sits some distance away from their other team-mate, or in another room.
2. Player one in the team has a 'house design sheet' and a pen/pencil.
3. Player one starts the game by deciding which room to designate first. For example, if he/she decides that the upstairs room on the right is the bedroom, he/she writes 'el dormitorio' or draws a picture of a bed inside that room.
4. When all the player ones from each competing team have made their decision the teacher tells the player twos to start.
5. Player two from each team visits his/her team-mate to find out which room has been chosen, while player three remains behind with a blank 'house design sheet'. On his return, player two tells player three what and where the room is on their design sheet, **in Spanish, not in English!** For example, in this case, they will need to point to the upstairs right room and say 'aquí está el dormitorio'. Player three must then write in the words 'el dormitorio', or draw an appropriate picture, in the correct room.
6. In the meantime player one chooses another room. Player two returns to player one to find out the whereabouts of the next room and returns to player three to relay that piece of information.
7. The winning team is the one who is first in relaying all the information correctly. Remind players that all of the information should be spoken in Spanish, and although a picture may be drawn instead, this will only take up extra time.

House design sheet

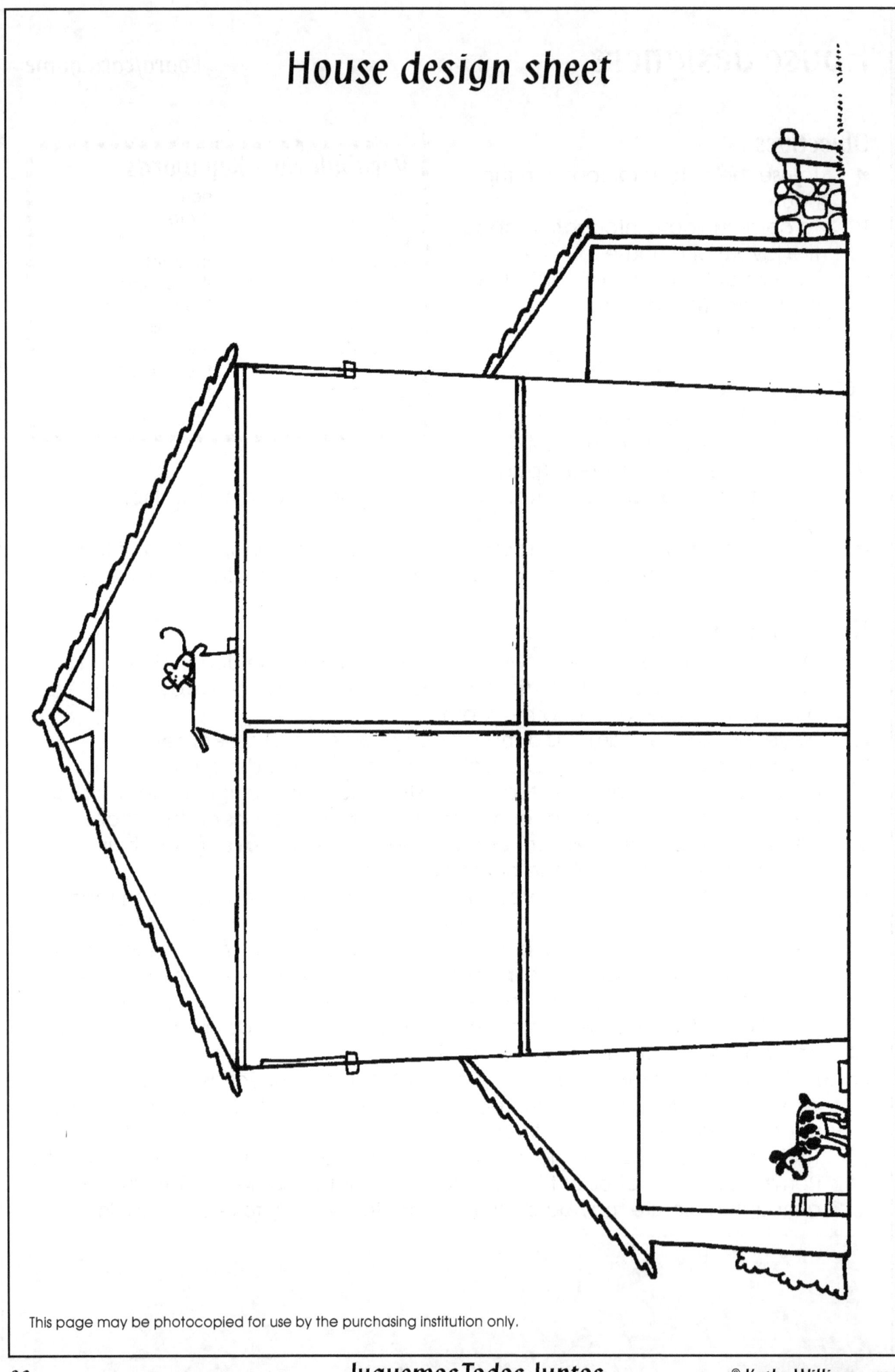

House designers room pictures

This page may be photocopied for use by the purchasing institution only.

Super sporty week

Board game

Objectives
- To prompt pupils to use the phrases 'hago ...' and 'juego a ...' in conjunction with seven sport activities
- To practise the days of the week (extension activity)

Setting up the game
- Play in pairs or small groups with one game board (page 33) per group.
- Dice and counters are required.
- Each pupil will need a week planner (page 34).

Vocabulario – Key words

hago ...	I do ...
ciclismo (m)	cycling
atletismo (m)	athletics
natación (f)	swimming
juego ...	I play ...
al fútbol (m)	football
al rugby (m)	rugby
al baloncesto (m)	basketball
al tenis (m)	tennis
lunes	Monday
martes	Tuesday
miércoles	Wednesday
jueves	Thursday
viernes	Friday
sábado	Saturday
domingo	Sunday

How to play the game
1. Starting at 'Comienza aquí' one pupil throws the die and moves the counter the relevant number of places around the board. They must **say** the phrase indicated by the activity picture on the place where they land. They then write the activity onto a day of their choice on the week planner. The next pupil then takes a turn and so on.
2. Pupils continue to throw the die in turn and move repeatedly around the board, until they have landed on all the activities and chosen which day to write them in. When they land on activities already used they must still say the appropriate sentence.

Extensions/variations
- You could make the game competitive by having a time limit, or by having the first player to complete their week as the winner. If you wish all pupils to complete the week plan, encourage those who have finished quickly to listen to and help the others, until all have finished.
- As a follow-up activity pupils could present their weekly activity plans to each other or the class, using for example: 'Los lunes hago atletismo. Los martes juego al fútbol.' etc.

Super sporty week board game

Comienza aquí ➡

This page may be photocopied for use by the purchasing institution only.

© Kathy Williams and Beatriz Rubio

Juguemos Todos Juntos

Super sporty week board game

lunes	
martes	
miércoles	
jueves	
viernes	
sábado	
domingo	

This page may be photocopied for use by the purchasing institution only.

Weather reporters

Board/card game

Objectives
- To ask and answer questions about the weather
- To reinforce the names of some principal towns in Spain

Setting up the game
- Pupils play together in pairs with one weather grid (page 36) each and a set of town and weather cards (page 37) per pair.

Vocabulario – Key words

hace sol	it is sunny
hace viento	it is windy
hace malo	the weather is bad
hace bueno	it is fine
hace calor	it is hot
hace frío	it is cold
llueve	it is raining
nieva	it is snowing
¿qué tiempo hace?	what's the weather like?
en	at/in

How to play the game
1. Put the town cards and the weather cards in two piles, face down.
2. Using the weather grids, both players first make a weather prediction for each of their towns and tell them to their partner in Spanish. They record their forecasts in writing or by drawing a picture in the 'weather forecast' column on the grid.
3. One player then picks up a town name card and asks what the weather is like there using 'Qué tiempo hace en …?' e.g. 'Qué tiempo hace en Barcelona?' The town card used is put to one side.
4. The other player picks a weather card and answers using the weather pictured, e.g. 'En Barcelona llueve.' The cards can be interpreted in a number of possible ways, for example the sun card could be 'Hace bueno / Hace sol / Hace calor.' If this is what either player predicted they put a tick in the second column; if they were wrong they put a cross. The weather card used is returned to the bottom of the pile.
5. The players swap roles and continue asking and answering until all the towns' weather conditions have been filled in on the grid.
6. The winner is the player who scored the most ticks at the end of the game.

Weather reporters town grid

Town	Weather forecast	✓ or ✗
Madrid		
Barcelona		
Valencia		
Bilbao		
La Coruña		
Sevilla		
Santander		
Toledo		

This page may be photocopied for use by the purchasing institution only.

Juguemos Todos Juntos

Weather reports

Barcelona	Bilbao	Sevilla	Toledo
Madrid	Valencia	La Coruña	Santander

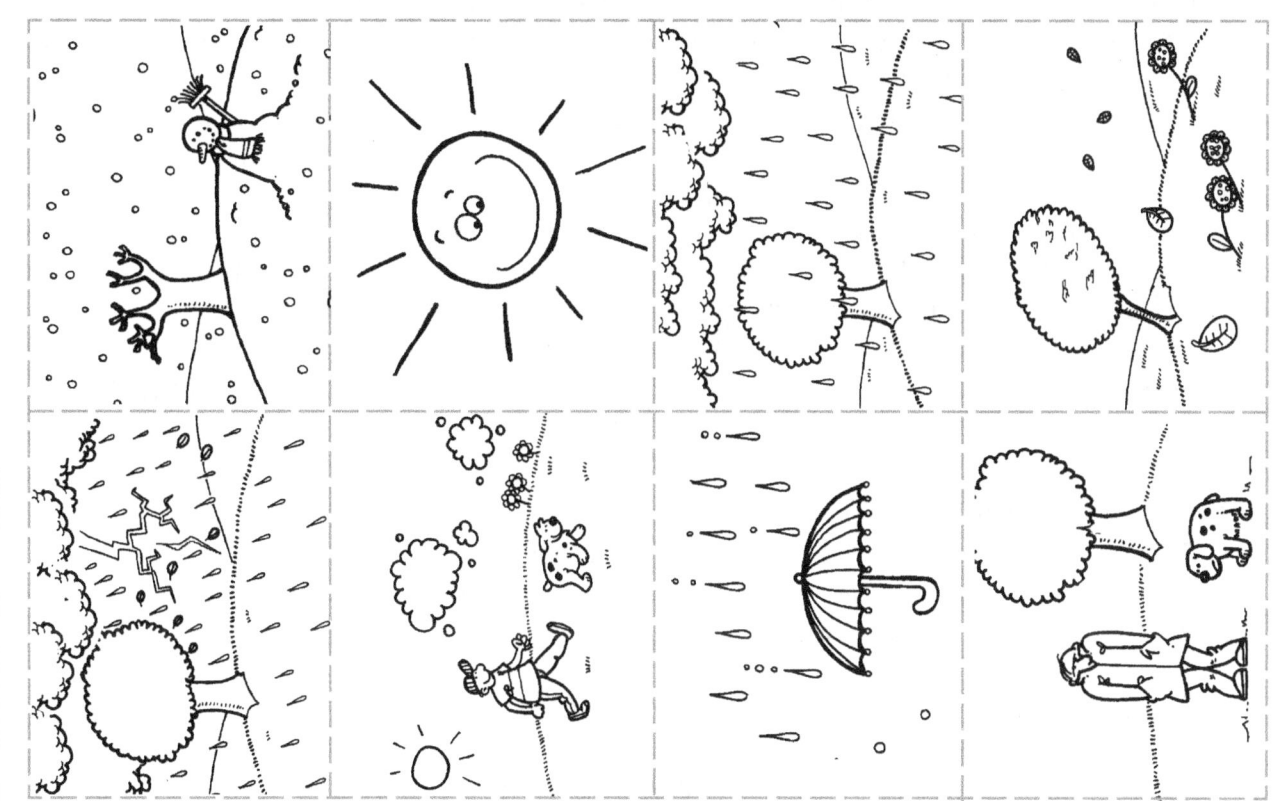

This page may be photocopied for use by the purchasing institution only.

Triple time

Card game

Objectives
- To practise telling the time in Spanish
- To reinforce understanding of digital and analogue times and the times written out in Spanish
- To revise the difference between 'es' and 'son' when talking about the time. 'Es' is used with one o'clock, and 'son' is used with all other times, e.g. 'Es la una', 'Son las dos', 'Son las tres', etc.

Vocabulario – Key words

es/son …	it is …
la una	one o'clock
las dos	two o'clock
las tres	three o'clock
las cuatro	four o'clock
las cinco	five o'clock
las seis	six o'clock
las siete	seven o'clock
las ocho	eight o'clock
las nueve	nine o'clock
las diez	ten o'clock
las once	eleven o'clock
las doce	twelve o'clock

Setting up the game
- Pupils work in pairs.
- Pupils need one set of time cards from page 39 per pair. You could make more cards to practise other times.

How to play the game
1. In pairs, players have a set of time cards in front of them, face down on the table.
2. One player turns over three different cards, trying to find a matching set of three. If he finds three which all say the same time – in digital, analogue and in Spanish – he keeps the set. If the three cards do not match, they are turned face down again and the other player has a turn. (The game works just like a 'pairs' game, except that the players are finding three cards.)
3. To aid the players' chances of finding a match, if they turn over two which match in one go, they keep these to one side until their next turn, when they have three chances to find the third card. If the third card is not found during that turn, they keep the pair to the side until the third is found on a further turn. If their opponent turns over the card that they are missing from their set, this card must be returned to the table, face down.
4. When the players are turning over the cards, encourage them to say the times out loud in Spanish every time, using a whole sentence, e.g. 'Son las cinco.'

Extension/variation
- The times are only on the hour, so that players can concentrate on their Spanish. You could make more cards which show half past, quarter to, etc. if you feel that your pupils can manage.

It is half past ten.	Son las diez y media.
It is quarter past three.	Son las tres y cuarto.
It is quarter to nine.	Son las nueve menos cuarto.
It is half past one.	Es la una y media.

Triple time cards

Set 1

Son las tres.	3:00	
Son las nueve.	9:00	
Son las once.	11:00	
Son las doce.	12:00	

Set 2

Son las ocho.	8:00	
Son las cuatro.	4:00	
Son las dos.	2:00	
Son las seis.	6:00	

This page may be photocopied for use by the purchasing institution only.

The best/worst day ever at school

Grid game

Objectives
- To practise saying school subjects
- To practise counting
- To practise saying times on the hour

Setting up the game
- Pupils need a 'school day timetable' (page 41) each and one 'Chinese counter' per pair (page 42). Cut out the grid and fold to make the counter.
- Pupils work in pairs.

How to play the game
1. Players fill in their 'ideal' timetable first in the right-hand column of the school day timetable sheet. They then fold back this column so that they cannot see the subjects they have written.
2. Player one picks a time for a lesson from his/her timetable at random, e.g. 'a las tres'.
3. Player two (who has the 'chinese counter') counts and moves the counter in and out **three** times, counting 'uno, dos, tres'.
4. Player one then picks one of the numbers visible on the counter, in Spanish, e.g. if five is visible he/she may pick that and say 'cinco'.
5. Player two counts and moves the counter again, this time **five** times.
6. Player one then chooses one of the visible numbers on the counter and this time player two lifts up the corresponding flap.
7. Under the flap is a school subject. Player one reads this out to player two, who then writes this into his/her timetable, in the hour that he/she originally chose (in this case 'a las tres'). Players must say out loud the timetable and subject as they fill this part in, e.g. 'A las tres tengo español.'
8. The players keep swapping over roles of choosing and counting so that both players can complete their timetables.
9. When all timetables are complete the class reveal and discuss their results. The best or worst school day!

Vocabulario – Key words
(el) español	Spanish
(el) dibujo	art
(el) inglés	English
(la) historia	history
(la) música	music
(la) informática	ICT
(las) matemáticas	maths
(las) ciencias	science
tengo	I have
uno	one
a la una	at one o'clock
a las dos	at two o'clock
tres	three
cuatro	four
cinco	five
seis	six
siete	seven
ocho	eight
nueve	nine
diez	ten
once	eleven
doce	twelve

Extension/variation
- The 'Chinese counter' is a very adaptable resource that can be used for counting practice as well as having different vocabulary written inside. For example, instead of school subjects, write in buildings. The day's timetable can be filled in to say the time that each building is visited on a tour of the town. Use 'visito …' instead of 'tengo …'

School day timetable

	tengo ...	tengo ...
a las 9		
a las 10		
a las 11		
a la 1		
a las 2		
a las 3		
a las 4		

Chinese counter template

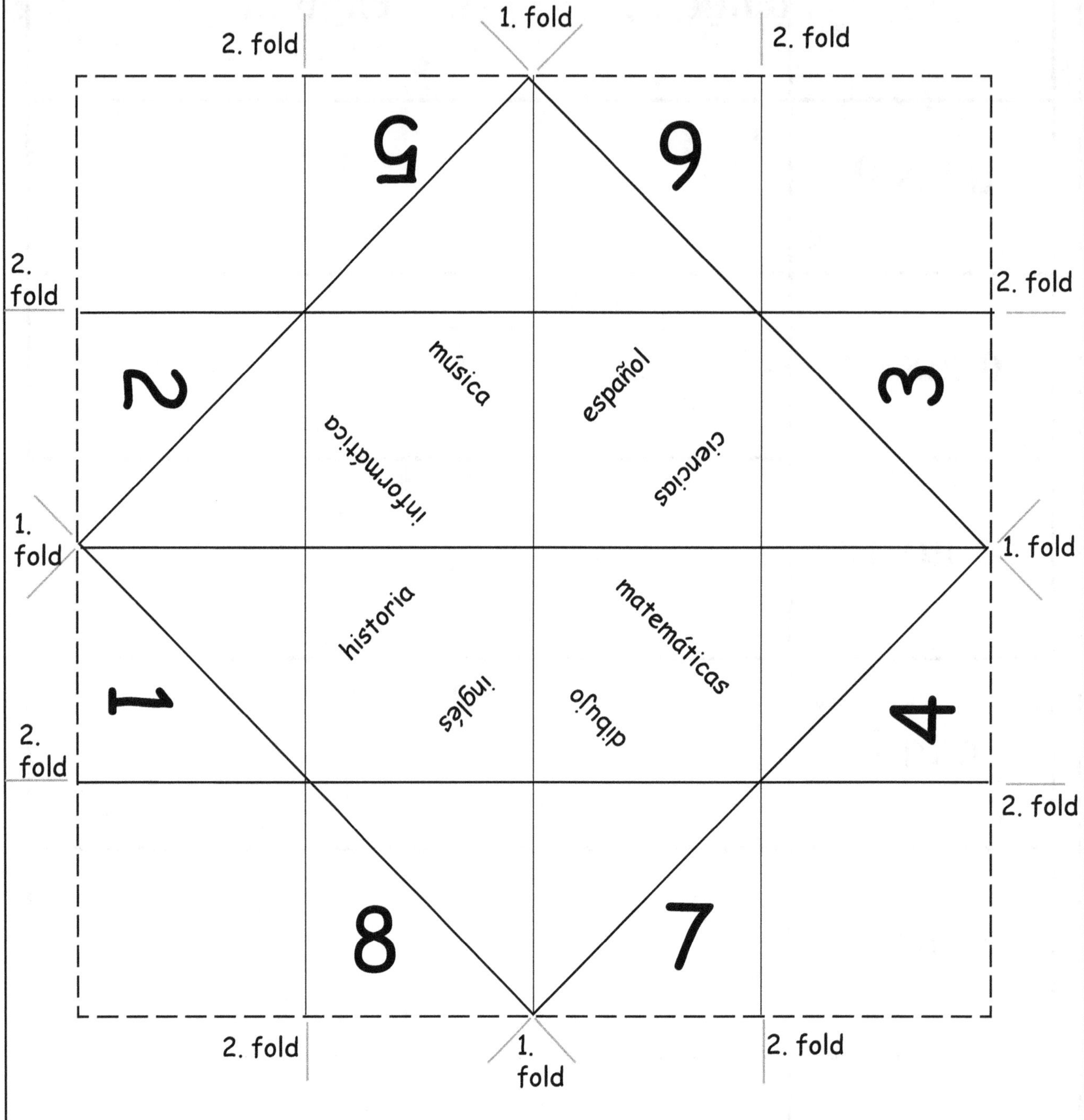

1. Fold corners **back** behind face of paper.
2. Fold corners **inward** to centre.
3. Put your thumb and forefinger of both hands into the back of the resulting square and pinch up into a point.

This page may be photocopied for use by the purchasing institution only.

Juguemos Todos Juntos

© Kathy Williams and Beatriz Rubio

www.brilliantpublications.co.uk

Like it or not

Board game

Objectives

- To practise saying 'me gusta/gustan …' and 'no me gusta/gustan …', while talking about school subjects
- To revise the use of 'me gusta/no me gusta …' with singular nouns, and 'me gustan/no me gustan …' with plural nouns (e.g. 'Me gusta la historia.' 'No me gustan las matemáticas.')

Vocabulario – Key words

me gusta/gustan …	I like …
no me gusta/gustan …	I don't like …
el español	Spanish
el dibujo	art
la educación física	PE
el inglés	English
la historia	history
la geografía	geography
la música	music
la informática	ICT
las matemáticas	maths
las ciencias	science

Setting up the game

- Pupils play in pairs using an enlarged photocopy of the grid (page 44), a coin, and a different coloured counter each.

How to play the game

1. The players put their counters on 'Comienza aquí'.
2. They decide who goes first by tossing a coin.
3. Player one tosses the coin – if **heads**, player one moves his/her counter to 'Me gusta/gustan …' completing the phrase with a school subject, for example, 'Me gusta la música.' If **tails**, player one moves to the 'No me gusta/gustan …' position instead, and completes the phrase accordingly.
4. Player two then tosses the coin and moves/speaks in the same way. Both players can be on the same place on the grid at the same time.
5. They continue to move across the grid until the first player reaches the last column on the right-hand side of the board. Player two must then throw the opposite to player one's last throw, and complete the opposite phrase to avoid losing the game. For example, if player one completed the course by throwing heads and said 'Me gusta/gustan …' then player two has to throw tails to finish, or he has automatically lost the game. If he throws tails then the game is a draw.
6. On completing the game, the players start again (and again) at 'Comienza aquí', with alternating players starting the game. They should keep a tally of how many games they win. They could play 'best of five' for example.
7. By repeating the game (at a quick pace for older pupils) the language is being continually reinforced. You could make it more challenging by saying that players must not repeat a school subject if their partner has already said it within that game. There are ten school subjects listed in the key words list, so this should be possible.

Extension/variation

- The game can be adapted to practise likes and dislikes of other things, e.g. different foods or sports.

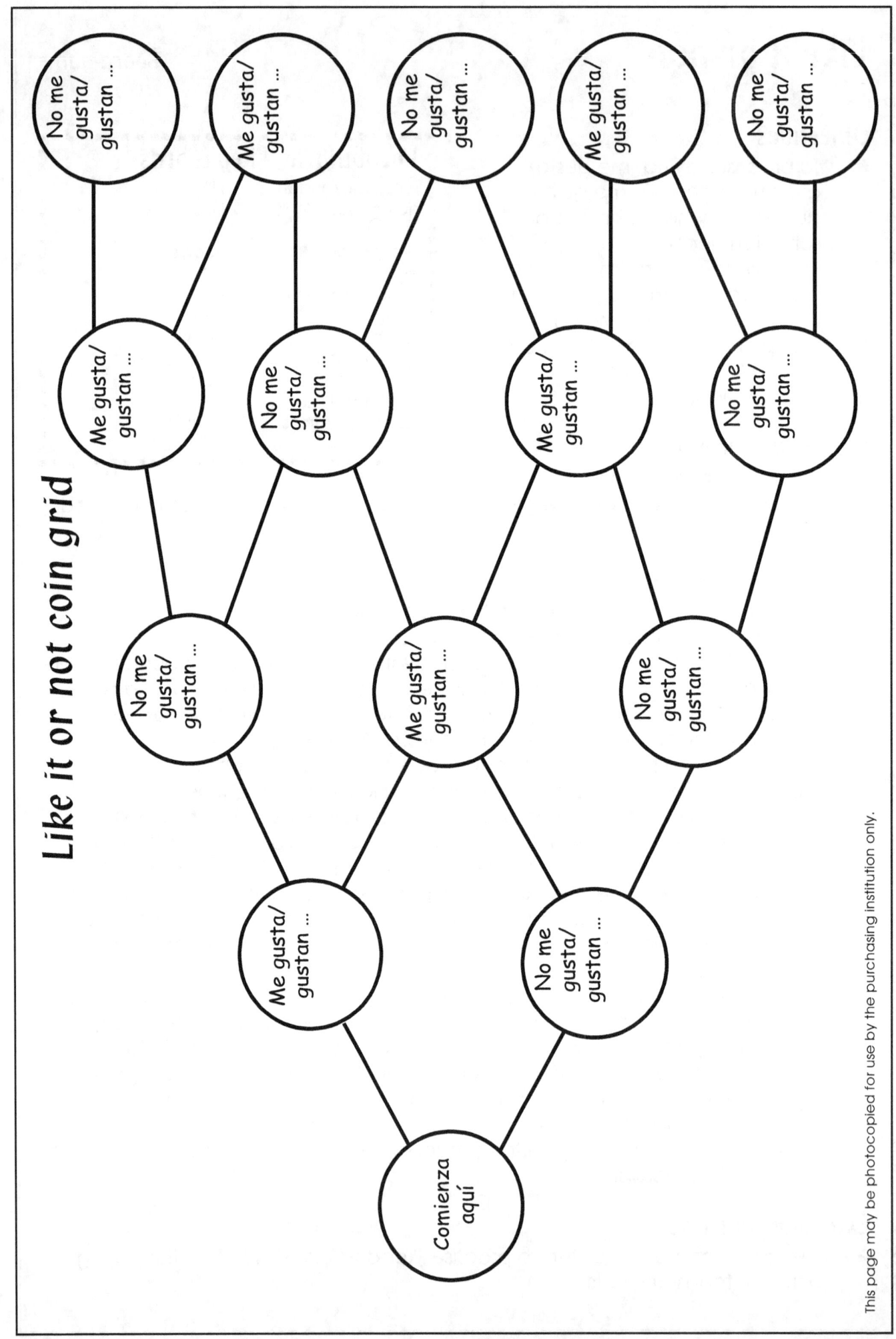

A tour of Spain

Board game

Objectives
- To practise using transport words
- To practise using 'Voy a + town'

Vocabulario – Key words
voy a …	I am going to …
	Madrid, Barcelona, Bilbao, etc.
en autobús	by bus
en barco	by boat
en bicicleta	by bike
en coche	by car
en avión	by plane
en tren	by train

Setting up the game
- All players require a map (page 47) each and one die between them, made from the template (page 48). This can be coloured and assembled in advance of the game by the players.
- The same game can be played either in pairs or groups of three or four.

How to play the game
1. Make sure all the players can identify the names of the main towns featured on the map before the game begins.
2. Each player must make a round trip of Spain, from Madrid back to Madrid, via the route shown on the map.
3. The players must keep their maps hidden from the view of the other player(s). This is because in the final part of the game, points are lost if two players have chosen the same form of transport for the same leg of the tour.
4. One player starts by rolling the die. He must say aloud the form of transport that he throws, and then quietly decide which part of the route he will make using that form of transport. It can be any leg of the journey that is chosen. For example, if he threw a train picture, he could decide to travel by train between Valencia and Málaga. He makes a note of his choice in the itinerary table below the map, and writes down the points he has scored using the die. Take care to fill in the correct line on the points tally.
5. The next player then throws the die, and makes a choice on his travel itinerary in the same way. The game continues until each player has made a complete route around Spain. They might have thrown the same picture most of the time and made almost the whole route by car, for example. Or they may have a wide variety of modes of transport in their travel itinerary. If, however, the boat is thrown, it can only be used between Barcelona and Valencia, Valencia and Málaga, or La Coruña and Bilbao. If they throw a boat and these legs of the journey have already been filled in, they have to miss a turn.

To score points
- Player one starts by saying in Spanish one of the sections of his journey, for example, 'Voy a Barcelona en coche.' The other player(s) look(s) at their maps, and if they have used the car for this section as well, then they all lose their points for this section. If only the first player has used the car here then he keeps his 1 point (on the die the car is worth 1 point).

© Kathy Williams and Beatriz Rubio

Juguemos Todos Juntos

- The next player then says one of her sections, 'Voy a Sevilla en tren.' The other players check their maps and either cross off their train and points, or leave other transport choices in place. As before, the player speaking only keeps her points if she is the only player to use the train in this part of the tour.
- When the whole route has been discussed, the winner is the player with the most points.

A tour of Spain

Voy a Madrid	en avión	4 points
Voy a La Coruña	....	___ points
Voy a Bilbao	....	___ points
Voy a Barcelona	....	___ points
Voy a Valencia	....	___ points
Voy a Málaga	....	___ points
Voy a Sevilla	....	___ points
Voy a Madrid	....	___ points

This page may be photocopied for use by the purchasing institution only.

Die template for a tour of Spain

This page may be photocopied for use by the purchasing institution only.

48
www.brilliantpublications.co.uk

Juguemos Todos Juntos

© Kathy Williams
and Beatriz Rubio

Quiz corners

Question and answer game/test

Objective
- To assess pupils' knowledge of several areas of language or vocabulary as a 'round-up' of a few weeks' work. The teacher can monitor answers orally during the game, or answers can be written down for the whole class to check at the end of the session.

Setting up the game
- In this game the questions can be in English so that the emphasis is on producing the right language in response, rather than trying to understand the question. Alternatively, as pupils become more knowledgable and confident, both questions and answers can be in Spanish.
- Photocopy and cut out the question vocabulary cards (page 50). Fill in the blanks to practise the particular area(s) of vocabulary that you want to assess. Alternatively, pupils could prepare these in advance for others in the class to use. If you play with just one set of cards, the pupils will have to return them so that other pairs/groups can also answer those questions. Alternatively, if you prepare several sets of cards, pupils could keep the cards and write their answers on them.
- Pupils work in pairs or small groups.

How to play the game
1. Designate the four corners of the classroom as the four 'quiz corners' (or if this is not feasible, four table tops, four trays or boxes). Using four separate areas makes it more interesting than a 'sit-down' test as pupils have to move between the areas and their 'bases'.
2. Name each corner with the first four letters of the Spanish alphabet.
3. Place an equal amount of cards in each of the four corners.
4. Player one chooses a corner at random. Player two has to pick up a card from there and ask player one the question written on the card. Player two then returns the card to the bottom of the pile he/she took it from (if you are playing with just one set of cards).
5. It is now the turn of player two to pick a corner, from which player one has to pick up a question card.
6. If the card chosen has already been answered, the players must still answer the question again before continuing. The fact that some cards may be repeatedly picked up in the attempt to find them all is beneficial as it gives pupils extra practice through repetition.
7. The game can be made competitive by setting a time limit within which the pair/group answering the most questions correctly wins. Alternatively the winning pair/group is the one which completes all the questions first.

Extension/variation
- Each corner could be used to practise a different theme, for example, weather in the 'A' corner, classroom items in the 'B' corner, days of the week in the 'C' corner, etc. Alternatively all the areas could have the same theme.

Corner question vocabulary cards

1. What is _____ in Spanish?	2. What is _____ in Spanish?	3. What is _____ in Spanish?
4. What is _____ in Spanish?	5. What is _____ in Spanish?	6. What is _____ in Spanish?
7. What is _____ in Spanish?	8. What is _____ in Spanish?	9. What is _____ in Spanish?
10. What is _____ in Spanish?	11. What is _____ in Spanish?	12. What is _____ in Spanish?

This page may be photocopied for use by the purchasing institution only.

Juguemos Todos Juntos

© Kathy Williams and Beatriz Rubio

Rock, paper, scissors

Question and answer game/test

Objective
- To test vocabulary or spelling using the 'rock, paper, scissors' hand game – more fun than writing down answers to a list of questions! (It can be used to practise any language area.)

Vocabulario – Key words
- roca (f) — rock
- papel (m) — paper
- tijeras (f, pl) — scissors

Setting up the game
- You can use the cards from 'quiz corners' (page 50) and the spelling cards (page 52). You will need two types of questions – ones which ask for an **oral response**, e.g. 'What is the Spanish word for "cheese"?' and ones which ask the players to **spell** a word, e.g. 'Spell the word for "cheese" in Spanish'. Alternatively questions can be in Spanish, e.g. '¿Cómo se dice "cheese" en español?' or '¿Cómo se escribe "cheese" en español?'
- Players sit in pairs around a table with the question cards in two piles in the middle. They need paper to record scores and for written responses.

How to play the game
1. On the count of three in Spanish they each put out one hand, with the hand made into one of three shapes – **rock** which is the fist clenched into a ball shape, **paper** which is a flat hand palm downwards, or **scissors** which is the forefinger and middle finger opening and closing (like scissors). If you wish, you could use the Spanish words for 'rock, paper, scissors' (see key words).
2. A player wins the round in the following ways:
   - 'paper' beats 'rock'
   - 'rock' beats 'scissors'
   - 'scissors' beats 'paper'
3. If both players have chosen the same hand shape, then there is no winner for that round and they must play again.
4. Whoever wins a round answers a question.
   - If he won using 'paper', his opponent asks him to **write down** a word.
   - If he won using 'rock', he has to **answer a question orally**.
   - If he won using 'scissors' he can cut his opponent's score back by one point, or he can opt for a question that his opponent chooses.
5. Answering questions correctly will get 2 points, incorrectly 0 points.
6. The winner is the player who has the most points at the end of a time limit, or when all the questions have been used up, whichever is most suitable.

Extension/variation
- Without using written question cards or point scoring, this game works well as a warm-up, a way of players testing each other orally on any subject they wish. It also works well as a time filler at the end of a lesson. Players do the 'rock, paper, scissors' actions and the winner answers questions as before, but they could be anything thought up by their partner, or from a particular theme or vocabulary list.

Spelling cards

1. How do you spell _____ in Spanish?	2. How do you spell _____ in Spanish?	3. How do you spell _____ in Spanish?
4. How do you spell _____ in Spanish?	5. How do you spell _____ in Spanish?	6. How do you spell _____ in Spanish?
7. How do you spell _____ in Spanish?	8. How do you spell _____ in Spanish?	9. How do you spell _____ in Spanish?
10. How do you spell _____ in Spanish?	11. How do you spell _____ in Spanish?	12. How do you spell _____ in Spanish?

This page may be photocopied for use by the purchasing institution only.

www.ingramcontent.com/pod-product-compliance
Lightning Source LLC
Chambersburg PA
CBHW081436300426
44108CB00016BA/2377